CAGED

CAGED

A TRUE STORY OF ABUSE, BETRAYAL, AND GTMO

LARA M. SABANOSH
FORMERLY LARA TUR

NEW YORK

LONDON • NASHVILLE • MELBOURNE • VANCOUVER

CAGED

A TRUE STORY OF ABUSE, BETRAYAL, AND GTMO

© 2022 **LARA M. SABANOSH**

Published in New York, New York, by Morgan James Publishing. Morgan James is a trademark of Morgan James, LLC. www.MorganJamesPublishing.com

This memoir depicts actual events in the life of the author as truthfully as recollection permits and/or can be verified by research and legal documentation. Occasionally, dialogue consistent with the character or nature of the person speaking has been supplemented. All persons within are actual individuals; there are no composite characters.

Morgan James BOGO™

A **FREE** ebook edition is available for you or a friend with the purchase of this print book.

CLEARLY SIGN YOUR NAME ABOVE

Instructions to claim your free ebook edition:
1. Visit MorganJamesBOGO.com
2. Sign your name CLEARLY in the space above
3. Complete the form and submit a photo of this entire page
4. You or your friend can download the ebook to your preferred device

ISBN 978-1-63195-539-6 paperback
ISBN 978-1-63195-540-2 eBook
Library of Congress Control Number:
2021902977

Morgan James PUBLISHING Builds with... Habitat for Humanity® Peninsula and Greater Williamsburg

Morgan James is a proud partner of Habitat for Humanity Peninsula and Greater Williamsburg. Partners in building since 2006.

Get involved today! Visit
MorganJamesPublishing.com/giving-back

To the two spirited women who have
given me the courage and motivation
to speak my truths—my daughters.

You have the most beautiful souls that capture the hearts
of those who cross your paths . . .
just as you did mine from the moment we met.

TABLE OF CONTENTS

ACKNOWLEDGMENTS

The experience of reliving the past twenty-five years of my life has been no short of a task. It has been a cathartic experience. A journey into a deeper part of my soul. Reliving memories—many that did not even make it into this book—has provided me with a chance to heal, as well as a chance to see a greater calling.

In this experience, I am so grateful for those that have been a part of my process. My journey was not made alone. I am blessed to have had people who have helped me get where I am today.

I want to thank my parents for their undeniable support. For never wavering. You are a model for everything I am to my children today. For every word, for every moment, I thank you.

I want to thank my daughters for your love and your belief in me. For your fighting spirits. For your courage and never giving up. I thank you both.

To my partner for loving me. You've never harbored judgments, remaining patient and supportive. Thank you for standing next to me, not in front of or behind me.

To my publisher, Morgan James Publishing, editor, Cortney Donelson, and marketing team—thank you for your guidance, wisdom, and expertise. You have empowered me beyond words. I am grateful for you all.

Lastly, in a strange kind of way, I thank all those who walked away from my children and me, those who chose gossip over friendship, and those who made judgments yet never asked questions. I thank you, too. I thank you for inspiring us to move forward. I thank you for empowering me to write this book. You motivated me to use my voice, the one I needed to tell my truth. I thank you all.

FOREWORD

I first met Lara in August 2013. I had just stepped off the plane into the oppressive Caribbean humidity after several days of travel and a final, far-too-early morning flight. I was tired, sweaty, and still questioning my choice to move far from family and friends for a victim advocate job at the isolated Guantanamo Naval Air Station.

Lara, by comparison, appeared unaffected by the heat and glamorous in her dark sunglasses and breezy white clothing. She immediately greeted me with a huge smile and, "Welcome to Gitmo! We're so glad you're here!" Her warm welcome and efforts to help me settle into work and community life over the next several months reaffirmed my decision to put my years of experience in civilian victim services to work for the military.

At first, Lara was my co-worker. She was eventually appointed to the director role at the Fleet and Family Support Center. In both roles, Lara was approachable, knowledgeable, and supportive of the entire staff. Our workplace felt like a family, and I credit Lara with fostering that environment.

Later, Lara was one of the victims with whom I worked. Victim advocates are trained not to discuss victim names or situations in public to protect victim safety and safeguard their confidentiality. Information about their experience is the victim's alone to share or not. Advocates stay in the background, supportive and silent. I only reveal my role in her experience with Lara's permission. Her story is still hers alone to share, which she does in this memoir.

As the child of a former military service member and as a former military spouse, I can say with confidence that domestic violence is not a new issue in the military. It is also not a small issue. According to a December 2019 report to Congress titled, "Military Families and Intimate Partner Violence: Background and Issues for Congress," there were 16,912 reported incidents in Fiscal Year 2018, and "there has been little change in the rate or number of reported incidents . . . since FY2009." In fact, there has been little change in more than twenty years, as there were more than 18,000 reports annually as far back as 2001. And these are just the reported incidents. The Bureau of Justice Statistics found that law enforcement is notified in only half of domestic violence incidents.

Lara's experience reveals the human side of these statistics. It also reveals a part of the domestic violence discussion that is frequently missed—abuse experienced by DoD (Department of Defense) civilian employees, contractors, and, in overseas locations, foreign national staff. These individuals make up a significant part of the overall DoD workforce but are rarely mentioned in reports and news articles or identified separately in military domestic violence statistics.

In the coming pages, Lara shares with you the fear, secrecy, and layers of abuse she experienced. Her words will resonate with those who have experienced domestic violence. What she shares also reveals her strength and resiliency. She is a survivor. I hope readers carry that fact with them after reading this book. For other survivors, I hope they are reminded of their own strength. I also hope that Lara's willingness to share her experience publicly inspires much-needed change in how the DoD addresses domestic violence. Improvements are long overdue. Lara, and every other victim, deserve for us to at least try.

Kristie M. Traver
Former Victim Advocate

PREFACE

"Insanity is relative. It depends on who has who locked in what cage."

—Ray Bradbury

They say every story has two sides. Aesop, the Greek fabulist, wrote in *The Mule*, "Every truth has two sides." It's time to tell the second side— my truth—of a grotesquely lopsided story that's been shared publicly for half a decade.

My silence up until now did not signal acquiescence but rather patience. *Caged: A Memoir of Abuse, Betrayal, and GTMO* is not a tell-all, though I suspect a few people will view it as such. But no. The truth is, I wrote this book to serve two purposes: to educate and embolden.

Caged is a window into the toughest moments of my life, moments no one should ever have to endure. But I did. And as with nearly all trauma, there is a measure of healing to be gained in sharing my story—healing for myself, my daughters, and others. I write to highlight the backstory of the main event, a tale that made headline news across the globe. The backstory, significant for understanding the whole picture, never seemed to make it past the media or any military records, not for lack of juicy details, but, I suspect, to protect a handful of people, subdue the pain of a grieving family, lift up the institution that is our military, and bow to tradition. I hope my words serve to educate and protect, too—protect a specific subgroup, which I will explain throughout these pages.

Integrity is a key theme of this story. Charles Marshall first used this definition of integrity, which was later made famous by C.S. Lewis: "Integrity is doing the right thing, even when no one is watching." The underlying premise is that an individual of integrity is of solid character. They are not doing the right things for rewards or praises but simply because they are the good and right things. There is a moral motive.

Finally, I imagine there will be a few military and history buffs who wish to read *Caged*. After all, Guantanamo Bay Naval Base, or GTMO, has always been the object of much speculation, curiosity, and gossip. I will do my best to accurately depict my perspective, realizing it's not the sole perspective, as long as readers understand I'm not an outlier, either. There are spouses at military bases all over the world who share a similar backstory. Maybe my words will empower others to seek out help or encourage those in positions of authority to assess existing procedures and question certain long-standing policies. This is the crux of my purpose in reliving this part of my life—to authentically write my story.

This is my *why*. Now onto the *what* and *how*. Let's dive in.

CHAPTER 1

THE WEIGHT OF SADNESS (PART I)

"Nobody understands another's sorrow, and nobody another's joy."
—Franz Schubert

January 11, 2015

"**M**rs. Tur, can you come help us out with the search?" Walter Bulnes's voice seems stern on the other end of the phone.

"Sure. No problem," I say. A dark feeling settles in the pit of my stomach. It has been two nights since Chris disappeared.

Kristie, the domestic violence liaison at the Fleet and Family Support Center, and I had just spent the night lying on the two couches in my living room. I can't sleep in my own bed. I can't sleep at all. My head throbs. My face is puffy. My anger from the past two nights has dissipated with the weight of Chris's lingering disappearance. But I'm not prone to worry. This is his modus operandi. He does this often—fleeing our home for the night in a drunken rage and failing to return until the next day. But two nights missing? That's new.

I arrive at the NCIS building—offices I know well from my work as a director on the Naval base at Guantanamo Bay in Cuba—and I'm guided to a small room. My teeth clench in anticipation. I recall the utter lack of professionalism I have encountered at NCIS over the years. I don't expect things to be different now.

In the past, the department head, Patrice Austin, a portly and bitter woman, whom I assumed had secured her job at GTMO as a last-place prize, much like being banished to Siberia, had said and done things to my clients that had stripped me of any feelings of respect toward her. As department heads, leaders should be confident, not frazzled and messy, which she often was. In cases where we had worked in tandem, I found her questions ludicrous, as if she didn't house a cell of empathy in her body. I knew of a couple of people at GTMO who had befriended her, but I was not one of them. In the past, I had even gone to NCIS to express my concern about her unprofessionalism. There had been no push back. Everyone had agreed with shoulder shrugs and head nods, yet nothing had changed.

Today would prove no different. She sits across from me in the white- and rubber-walled room. She and Walter give me the run-down, one which, later, I'd discover was not only inappropriate but outright unethical.

"This isn't an interrogation. We just want your help."

"Okay," I reply, feeling every ounce of the fatigue two nights with little sleep can produce. As I sit looking at Patrice, I think how now it's my turn to be her next victim. I feel like just another case for her to chew on and spit out.

Patrice and Walter don't tell me they are recording our conversation, and I see no video cameras sporting red lights. They also fail to tell me my words are considered *under oath*. Later, I would discover they had secretly recorded our conversation, and it was, indeed, investigative in nature.

Patrice asks, "Why have you stayed all these years?"

I stare at her in disbelief and shake my head in disgust at her ignorance. Sarcasm is much easier to choose than sitting in and feeling the pain of anguish. What answer could she possibly hope to hear?

I like getting punched in the face. That's why I stay. My thoughts pepper my brain, and I know they sound impatient. I take a deep breath.

"I don't know." It's an easy answer for a difficult time.

Patrice stands up and moves in and out of the room repeatedly. I provide all the whereabouts Chris had chosen during his previous forays to Walter, but she is distracting me with her coming and going. Anger swells, and my neck feels warm. This conversation sure seems more like an interrogation with each passing minute.

Walter appears frustrated with me, and I don't know why. I assume it's because he's been friends with Chris for years. Chris, as the Navy Exchange Loss Prevention manager, helps NCIS with their camera systems. I believe they've gone fishing together, too. I imagine it's difficult to handle a missing person's case when the missing person is your buddy. As Walter eyes me for the tenth time, I briefly think there must be a conflict of interest somewhere.

Patrice enters the room again from a longer-than-usual break.

"We're done. We need to stop. Lara, can you come with me? You can leave your stuff," she says. NCIS agents buzz me through a door, and I realize we're moving toward a conference room. I've been here before, helping clients and their families.

When they open the double doors to the conference room, I immediately know: My life will be forever changed. I know, somewhere in the recesses of my heart, that Chris is dead.

Captain J.R. Nettleton, the commanding officer, or CO as he's often called, stands in full dress uniform. He is flanked by perhaps a dozen people, including the casualty assistance calls officer, otherwise known as the CACO, the base's general manager, representatives from the Navy Exchange, and others in uniform.

"I'm so sorry, but we found your husband's body this morning—" the CO begins.

I crumble to a nearby chair. Sobs erupt from my throat, and all I can think about is how sad I feel. Everything else goes numb. My peripheral vision evaporates, but it doesn't matter. Tears block my vision. I hear others speaking, but their muffled voices offer no solace: "I'm sorry," they say.

Twenty years of marriage is a long time. Chris is a part of me, and I feel as if a piece of me has just died. My sorrow isn't because I just lost the love of my life. My sobbing isn't in response to learning my best friend has passed away. I am sad because even though I hate what Chris has done to me, and I hate what he put our family through, I never wanted him dead. For the past two nights, in my mind, our relationship was over. He is toxic, but I don't hate him. I never hated him.

A thought travels on repeat through my head: "He needs help, yes. But he doesn't deserve to *not* be here." My mind is still thinking about Chris in the present tense. I can't believe what's happening. *Chris can't be gone* . . .

Captain Nettleton says, "I don't want to rush you, Lara, but we all know how quickly word spreads here. I want you to be able to get home to tell your daughters before they hear it from someone else."

He's right. At GTMO, even though we're not technologically advanced, gossip travels faster than social media. The chaplain moves toward me and helps me stand. My legs threaten to buckle at any moment, but somehow, I follow him outside the NCIS building.

CHAPTER 2

SMITTEN

"When you fall head over heels for someone, you're not falling in love with who they are as a person; you're falling in love with your idea of love."

—Elisabeth Rohm

Winter 1994

I was a second-year college student, home from school during Christmas break and attending a party in a suburb of Philadelphia, when I met Chris Tur for the first time. I was barely nineteen years old.

He stepped into the room where I stood with some of my girlfriends, wearing only a towel around his waist.

He cursed and escaped back into the bathroom, slamming the door, clearly unhappy to see three underaged girls standing outside his bathroom. I froze, insecurity clamping my feet to the floor. Unsure if anyone even wanted us there, I felt silly.

Nonetheless, my friends and I stayed. Compared to the typical college guys I partied with, Chris was different. A little rough around the edges, arrogant yet nice, and fun in a way I had yet experienced. I was used to frat houses and hanging around people who were all the same age. After only a few months away at college, boredom had set in. My friends and I sought out activities and co-eds at other schools to break up the monotony, but it was the same people all the time, even if the names and faces differed at each campus.

So this military guy—a six-foot-tall Marine with conviction and bravado—interested me as no one else had. I liked how he smelled, a mixture of soap and spice. Even though he had given me a fake name that first night we met, as he did with many of the other girls before me, I was quickly swept away. That he'd lie about who he was mesmerized me. And yet, this liar was still kind. Over the next couple of weeks during the holiday season, he showed more interest in me, making me feel as if I was the only one in a room full of people. I fed off the attention.

His delight in me, my infatuation with him, and my naïveté collided. At nineteen, I didn't know what to look for in a relationship, nor what to look out for. Dancing around my immaturity, we started a more serious dating relationship, even though we barely saw each other once we returned to our respective lives. Me to school. He to Camp LeJeune in North Carolina.

Neither of us could stand the distance, so not long after the Christmas break, I chose to forgo my college experience, and I moved back in with my parents to be "closer" to where he was stationed, even though I was still living a few states away.

Chris drove the eight hours back to Pennsylvania, where his family lived as well, every weekend to stay with me at my parents' house while we were dating. I thought this was incredibly romantic. My feelings for him and our relationship grew.

When you fall in love, it's a little like going mad. You can't think straight. You make poor choices. You're not yourself. And that's how it was for me during our short dating relationship. Because Chris was fun and intoxicating to be around, I found myself losing a bit of my identity because I wanted so badly to be wrapped up in his exciting world and not my old, routine existence. Yet, he felt safe. I didn't wish to be around anyone else.

Looking back, I realize I was driven by the idea of this new relationship and wasn't thinking about my best interests or long-term plans. It wasn't that I hadn't dated anyone before, but I did not have a long list of former boyfriends. Living in the moment, I was like a little girl in a big girls' world. I was trying to "adult," and I wanted to be an adult, but I wasn't very good at it. I wasn't worldly or somebody who had been with many guys, if you know what I mean. And per my request, Chris was patient in that regard, too, which just solidified my respect for him.

Chris's family was kind but different from my family. For one, the Tur family was larger. I only have my parents and a younger brother. Chris was one of four kids, sliding in line as the youngest. The Tur family was louder, too—likely a byproduct of such a large group. Two of his brothers were already married with children, and his grandmother lived with them. He just seemed to exist in a different world than me. With all the noise came activity. I experienced more excitement and movement with his family than I ever had before.

Chris and his sister didn't seem to get along well. The first time I met her, she burped in my face. I found it immature, so the fact the two didn't spend a lot of time together didn't bother me. He seemed to prefer spending time with his brothers.

After seven months of distance dating, I went on vacation with Chris and his family to Hilton Head Island. His sister didn't come. It would be the first time I witnessed Chris get angry with his family and the first tangible confirmation I received that his family dynamics functioned much differently than mine.

Halfway through the week, we sat on the balcony of the vacation house—Chris, his parents, his brothers, and me. I knew from anecdotes here and there that poking fun at each other in the Tur household was a common pastime. This time, they targeted Chris, and he didn't take it well. After several requests to stop—to no avail—he stood up and yelled the f-word to his family, slammed the door, and walked away. I was left staring at everyone, unsure what to do. His mom laughed, and one of his brothers turned to me and said, "Welcome to the Addams Family," smirking as if the family secret was now out.

Minutes turned into an hour, and Chris was still gone. No one seemed to care. No one asked about him or made any effort to find him. Even after Chris finally returned hours later, everyone acted as if nothing had happened. I expected apologies or at least some discussion about what had happened. But there was nothing. It was then I learned this chiding and picking on people was normal, even acceptable, in his family, and I didn't like it. It seemed to me there was a broad lack of respect for each other. But only seven months in, who was I to judge? I simply moved forward.

As the months passed, our relationship grew even more serious. Chris talked about his upcoming deployment to Okinawa, Japan. Every time he did, heaviness seemed to fill my lungs. Trying to remain positive and upbeat, I blinked away the tears that threatened to form. Without consciously realizing it, I had become so attached to this complicated man that I no longer knew how to do life without him.

I don't know who brought it up first, but the idea of secretly getting married entered our conversations. Both of our fathers were former military, so it would be impossible to take a military flight with him to Japan. Everyone would find out. Nonetheless, we went ring shopping and continued dreaming. Chris wasn't able to afford a ring himself yet, so I co-signed for it. This kind of shopping reminded me that I was more old-school than I realized. While there are some wedding traditions that go in and out of style, there's one that never will: Asking your future wife's parents for their blessing. I confided in Chris that I wanted him to ask my dad for "permission" to marry me. He agreed.

Fall 1995

Chris's deployment was scheduled for late December. It was November 20, my birthday, and we had made reservations at an elegant restaurant. I slipped on some fancy clothes and spent more time than usual on my hair. I suspected this would be the night Chris proposed.

At dinner, Chris turned to me and said, "I'm sorry . . . but I never got a chance to talk to your dad."

Tears threatened to spill. The moment most girls dream about—me included—felt destroyed by so many conflicting emotions.

I guess tonight's not the night, I thought, disappointed. I didn't want to be inappropriate or ruin the evening, so I rose from my chair to go to the restroom and gather myself so we could enjoy the rest of my birthday. As soon as I stood up, Chris moved from his chair and bent down on one knee in the middle of the restaurant.

I consider myself a private person, and here, the entire restaurant stared at me in anticipation. My eyes were already moist because I thought he couldn't talk to my dad so our engagement would be delayed. But at that moment, I realized, despite my wishes, he was still going to propose.

Without feeling I had an option to do anything else, I heard myself say, "Yes."

Hollywood provides us with such lofty ideals and expectations around marriage proposals and weddings. I likely fell into that trap of fantastical thinking. In doing so, I had set myself up for disappointment.

It was my twentieth birthday, but the waitstaff brought champagne. Everyone clapped. I couldn't decide if I was elated or crushed, full of joy or harboring the first inklings of resentment. Not wanting to seem ungrateful, I stuffed my swirling emotions and remembered that I loved this man, and as we had planned for months, we were now going to get married! We celebrated for a bit at the restaurant and then went to share the news with our families.

Everyone seemed happy, including me. With my family's excitement, I was able to let go of the disappointment that Chris hadn't talked to my dad first. With hope, I looked forward to our future together.

Much later, I discovered Chris had been joking the night of his proposal. He had talked to my dad first and was kidding when he said he hadn't. *Joking.* That was Chris. His mean-spirited jokes, which I never found funny, were now more often aimed at me instead of his family and friends. Once, I asked him to stop, explaining I was too sensitive to find them humorous, but he didn't listen. If I tried to joke with him, he waved me off and called me a "psycho." During these months, I learned first-hand that adding "just kidding" after a rude or belittling comment doesn't make the statement okay. It still stings.

I had been dealing with what I thought was an ulcer that whole week, so the following day, I had a doctor's appointment to get checked out. I was experiencing awful heartburn. It was the Wednesday before Thanksgiving. I was also determined to attend a party at a friend's house that night. The party would give me a chance to show my friends my engagement ring.

The doctor ran some tests and said the lab would call with the results. She suspected I was pregnant and didn't trust the negative urine tests. I laughed at the idea. I was on the birth control pill. "It's stress," I assured her. "I am working, taking classes, and my new fiancé is about to be deployed." I shook my head at the possibility of a baby.

A few hours later, when I arrived at the party, one of my friends confided in me that I looked pregnant when I told her I hadn't been feeling well. I laughed at her, too. But on top of that, the evening was a mixed bag of emotions anyway. Some of my friends were less than excited about my engagement. They thought I was too young. They were attending college and on different life tracks than the one on which I suddenly found myself as a fiancé and soon-to-be military wife. In hindsight, I've learned it's easy to see the flaws in others' plans but not so much in your own.

Sure enough, on Black Friday, while on vacation at a house in the Pocono mountains with Chris's brothers and their wives, my blood work came back: "Baby on board."

If it's possible to be both thrilled and terrified, I suppose I was. We confided in our families that we were expecting, and everyone was supportive. Chris was most excited about the news, and his positivity fueled my high expectations. I assumed my life was falling into place sooner than I imagined, but it would all be amazing. I was truly an "adult" now!

We didn't share the news with anyone else. With our recent engagement and his deployment, we knew our pregnancy wouldn't be widely accepted by most people. He was leaving for Japan for an entire year, but I knew I could join him soon if we were married. Even the wedding announcements in the newspapers mentioned such plans.

We rushed to hold our wedding within two weeks, and Chris and I were married in mid-December. It was a beautiful wedding, even though it was mostly held for our families' benefit. I felt a bit indifferent about the whole ceremony since Chris and I were in our own little world. When it had been time to find bridesmaids' dresses, I wasn't even there. I struggled between joy and sadness and often felt disconnected as I wrestled with conflicting emotions. I would try to speak up, but I didn't think anyone was listening. So I became the happy bride on the outside while inside, I embraced the feelings of being lost and alone. In the end, I couldn't believe we pulled off the wedding; it wouldn't have happened without the help of so many of our family members.

Because Chris was leaving the country, we never planned a honeymoon. We figured we could celebrate in Japan. And his family wanted to spend time with him before he deployed anyway.

It wasn't until a month later, after Chris was settled in Okinawa, that he let me know I could not join him on base. He explained I couldn't be added to his orders because I wasn't allowed to give birth in a military hospital. So I was forced to stay home and live with my parents. I missed Chris dearly. Honestly, that longing to be with my husband was covered with a bit of resentment since his parents had requested so much time with him after our wedding—time that now, I wished I had soaked in.

CHAPTER 3

THE IDEA OF LOVE

"If you don't stand for something, you will fall for anything."
—Gordon A. Eadie

Summer 1996

At first, Chris and I spoke on the phone every night. The expense of these long-distance calls (before international cell phones made it simpler) was absurd. Our phone bills looked more like mortgage payments. We also sent letters back and forth—nearly weekly.

The months crept along, and my stress level rose as our communication waned. I was working as a bank teller and attending classes. I suppose the novelty of being newlyweds gave way to the challenges of a long-distance relationship.

During those months, I picked a place for us to live, securing an apartment I thought we could call home, though it wasn't in the most desirable neighborhood. Money was tight, so I did the best I could. Chris's parents bought us furniture for our wedding, so I went to work picking out our bedroom set and baby furniture. My opinion didn't matter much. Ann, Chris's mom, kept telling me why everything I picked was wrong. I know it's typical mother-in-law/daughter-in-law woes, but when your husband is so far away, it makes for a lonely backdrop. As I set everything up, I felt a bit like I was playing "house," given my new husband wasn't there to help, and I was still only twenty.

As my due date approached, there were problems with the pregnancy. My doctors drew up a Red Cross message for Chris. They believed he should come home because they didn't think I'd make it to my original due date.

The military granted him leave, and my dad and I went to pick him up at the airport. My dad offered to let me walk ahead to have a moment alone with Chris as soon as he stepped off the plane. As Chris walked down the terminal hallway, I opened my arms, and he walked right past me.

When Chris had left in December, I had long, blonde hair and was fairly fit. At seven months pregnant, I had gained fifty pounds and now wore my hair short. And I sported new glasses. He hadn't recognized me as I waddled toward him. My dad laughed and pointed back behind Chris when Chris asked him where I was. "You just missed her."

When Chris turned around and saw me, he only said, "Oh!" I can't say I blamed him. I didn't look anything like I did when he had left for Japan. It was the middle of the summer heat, I was toting extra weight from my pregnancy, and all I wanted was to deliver our daughter and start our lives.

Chris was exhausted from the jetlag and months spent living as an active Marine. When we arrived at our apartment, he took a slow look around.

"I don't like this bedding. You have to take it back." They were the first words out of his mouth. It wasn't just the bedding. He criticized the apartment and the furniture, too. I knew his taste was different from mine and we had limited resources, but I agreed to change the bedding. I wanted to start off on the right foot, still flying on the happy feelings of finally having my husband home.

"I planned a welcome home party with all your friends. They've missed you." I told him.

The party was short-lived. Chris wasn't interested at all, and not long after everyone arrived, he asked them to leave. That was the end of his welcome home party.

I justified the terse behavior. He was tired. I was tired. My excitement waned and morphed into disappointment. *This is not how I pictured all this would go!* We were both wrestling with the stress of becoming new parents and figuring out how to be married, even though we were nearly eight months into it. The sense of security I had felt with Chris before we had married was gone, and confusion and concern crept in.

A week or two later, we started to slide into a groove, but then the arguments started. Doctors had limited me to bed rest, yet I still had to work. Chris had no job, and as the days turned into weeks, his unsuccessful job search taxed our relationship. He flip-flopped between odd jobs, trying to earn some money.

On July 16, we went in for a doctor's appointment. Chris has been home only a few weeks. At the appointment, the doctors determined I was in the early stages of labor. I was leaking amniotic fluid. My body was ready. Our daughter was not. Nonetheless, we prepared to return to the hospital the next morning so labor could be induced.

At midnight, I started to leak a lot of fluids, and we returned to the hospital where they hooked me up to monitors. By morning, I was on my way to an unscheduled C-section. Chris was beside me the whole time, including when we returned home with our daughter—Savannah.

As I mended, Chris did the heavy lifting around the house, getting up at night with Savannah, and taking care of me. I felt lucky and very much cared for. Yet, I still slipped into postpartum depression. My emotions jumped all over the place. Then, so did Chris's. Savannah had colic and cried constantly. We were not sleeping.

Chris lost his tolerance for anything and stopped nurturing Savannah. Thankfully, we had family in the area, and they often helped us with meals, cleaning, and taking care of our new baby. It seemed to me Chris had gone through a transformation, one that would soon bring me to the darkest depths of my soul.

After Savannah's arrival and many failed attempts to secure employment, Chris started a job with a landscaping business to help our little family make ends meet. I offered whatever help I could and made him bagged lunches to take on the job. Given our financial strain, I rotated four basic ingredients: peanut butter, jelly, bananas, and fluff.

On one particular day, I made him a plain peanut butter sandwich, something I had often eaten as a child. When Chris arrived home after work, he threw the sandwich at me and screamed, "Who would make a peanut butter sandwich for someone working outside all day?" He accused me of trying to kill him and cursed at me. "If you're going to make me lunch, you better do it right!"

"It's not my job to make you lunch," I tried to keep my reply simple.

"If your fat (insert explicative) is going to stay home, it *is* your job!"

He's right. I've failed.

Even though I believed Chris's put-downs, my parents had never spoken to each other like this. Tears sprung from my eyes, even as I fought to hold them back. Chris walked out of the door. From that point forward, I did everything I could to make sure I wasn't on the receiving end of that kind of outburst again. I was unsuccessful.

Our confrontations became a constant part of the culture in our home. His way of coping with conflict was to either run away or fight, quite literally. I was still trying to lose the fifty pounds I had gained with Savannah, and breastfeeding was not easy. Often, Chris used the words, "a lazy fat a$$" to describe me. It seemed they were the first words out of his mouth whenever he was unhappy. With postpartum depression and this onslaught of verbal abuse, darkness permeated my days. I learned that the more I cried, the longer the verbal attack would last.

Over the weeks, emotional numbness set in. If I went inward, Chris would stop the insults, so with each instance, that's what I learned to do—dive down into myself and wait for the storm to pass.

Then the physical abuse started.

We were in our apartment, getting ready to leave for an errand. I was placing Savannah in her car carrier, which sat on the carpet. Chris was in my face, yelling. I wanted him to back up, but he wouldn't, so I grabbed a wad of his hair and demanded he get out of my space. In response, Chris grabbed me around my neck and threw me to the floor. My head made contact with the concrete hidden under the cheap carpet. With his hands still wrapped around my windpipe, he screamed, "Don't ever (explicative) touch me again! Ever!"

Terror didn't just creep in, it flooded my whole being. The trust and safety I once felt at his hands evaporated. My heart raced and all thinking ceased. Throughout the entire year we had dated, Chris had never become angry with me, and I hadn't seen this side of him before. Yes, we fought, but words were words. I didn't know what to do. So I froze, feeling powerless and ashamed, hoping and praying if I went limp, he'd stop the chokehold. My insides squeezed with physical and emotional pain. I didn't dare cry out. That would have been worse. I no longer felt like an adult, but a helpless child. *Child.*

What about Savannah? My brain woke up.

At that point, one of my girlfriends walked in and diffused the situation. She ordered us to stop fighting, and breathlessly, we did. As I stood up, I also crawled into myself even further. *I don't know how I'm going to keep doing this.* Even though, on some primal level, I realized he was responsible for his verbal tirade and frightening physical reaction, I blamed myself. I had grabbed his hair. I had set him off.

"I'm so sorry, Chris. You're right. I'm having a hard time right now. This is my fault." At the time, his yelling in my face, lashing out with his tongue, and the name-calling seemed insignificant. Looking back, I realize I wanted so badly to have the wonderful little family I had envisioned, I was willing to do whatever it took to make it happen. Whatever it took—*to a point.*

Before I realized it, a year went by, and we moved out of that apartment and into our first house.

———————

Summer 1997

Chris and I moved into a quad home—a townhome that backed up to others rather than sit in a row—and that had a common area in the middle. It was three levels, which included a finished basement and a deck, giving us room to grow as a family. I was in love with our first house.

I assumed now that we owned something, it meant a chance to start over. A new chapter awaited. I had been working as a teller at a local bank and had recently moved up to the position of branch manager and loan officer. Even the local paper cited my success as "The Fastest Moving Young Professional in Finance." Our money stress eased a bit.

However, the hours were not conducive to our family's needs. During the evenings, I attended events at the Chamber of Commerce as part of my job or took classes toward my degree. Chris complained about my absence. To be fair, household things weren't getting done: laundry, cooking, and cleaning. Our arguments continued. I didn't want to be a failure, but I didn't know what to do to remedy the situation. I slapped on a fake smile and charged forward, keeping up a false narrative to the best of my ability. I didn't want the rest of the world to know I was a failure, too.

Chris was still bouncing around jobs rather unsuccessfully. When he was bored, there were times he showed up unannounced at my office. I found it unprofessional, and I imagine my coworkers did as well. The whole dynamic wasn't working for me. Despite my quick advance up the financial industry ladder, I made the difficult decision to leave my career.

Instead, I accepted assignments through a temporary agency, which afforded me the chance to work normal eight-to-four or nine-to-five hours and secure health insurance. I could be there for Savannah, easily schedule doctors' appointments, and if needed, be available for Chris.

Chris continued to go out with friends to parties, even though our finances were limited again. He wanted to do what he always did. His drinking ratcheted up a notch. Financial and relational stress levels also climbed again in our home. He wanted to keep up the appearance that we had plenty of money. Even though his dad had held high-level jobs in the finance industry, *budget* wasn't a word Chris liked to hear. I decided to look for more permanent work to relieve some of the burden.

I landed a job with a pharmaceutical company in the technology department. Again, I made decent money, and within the same company, Chris found a job, too. We worked at two different locations, so we weren't on top of each other all the time. That and the steady stream of two incomes were a nice reprieve.

1999

When Savannah was three years old, we started talking about having another baby. She was in preschool, and I felt as if I could finally breathe a bit. As our discussions progressed, I told Chris that if we had two children, I didn't necessarily want to work because I knew it would take a lot of time to raise two children and keep the house up. I never wanted to be a housewife but a mom, yes—always. We did have the help of our families, but my mom was going back to work more hours and his dad was retiring, so we didn't have reliable childcare. I knew if I worked, our lives would dive back into chaos. Any mom knows how taxing it can be to figure out the logistics of transportation, meal planning and prep, and having two young children while working full-time.

It wasn't long before I was pregnant. All through the pregnancy, Chris proved he still wasn't inclined to back away from his extracurricular activities or worry about the growing amounts of our debt or bills. I was responsible for keeping tabs on preschool tuition and preparing for a new baby and all the financial commitment that brings.

The abuse continued as well. One day, he hit me in my stomach, and I had to cancel an appointment with my obstetrician because he had left a bruise. I just kept hiding everything he was doing to me.

When Madison was born, Chris's lifestyle continued to mirror that of a bachelor's rather than a father of two. Chris still worked at his job, so there was no reason we couldn't afford everything we needed, at least in his mind. But I watched our money leak out of our account as he frequented bars and other places with his friends at night, and I became resentful. It came to the point where we needed to take out a second mortgage because we were enjoying vacations and living via our credit cards rather than being responsible. I say "we" because I wanted the vacations, too. I also didn't want to rock the boat.

We did pay off much of our debt with the second mortgage, including my wedding ring and other items I discovered Chris had never paid for. When I confronted him with the number of charge-offs and a second ring he had purchased with credit, he scratched his head and simply said, "I thought I had paid for that." I felt annoyed, but I justified it with the fact I had incurred student loans. I felt I had no room to complain.

We paid off the credit cards and tried to start over. My optimism rose. It seemed we were at a new crossroads, and I hoped things would change. It was a new millennium (2000), we had a new baby and felt complete as a family of four, and our financial slate had been wiped clean. *Where might we go from here? The sky's the limit. What could go wrong?* I was about to find out.

CHAPTER 4

ALL KINDS OF ABUSE

"Integrity means that you are the same in public as you are in private."

—Joyce Meyer

Ring. Ring . . . Ring. Ring.

"Hello."

"Hey, Lara. I just got a DUI."

Since we had been married and he had returned from Japan, he had never called me by any term of endearment. No *honey*. No *babe*. No *sweetie*. Just Lara. As if I was a roommate or coworker.

Since marriage, we had also agreed on this rule: no driving drunk. I told him what seemed to be a thousand times that I would always come get him if he had consumed too many—that he should never drive home with even a buzz. It was too risky. Aside from DUIs, he could be involved in accidents or worse—kill himself or someone else. The inconvenience factor of dropping everything to pick him up from a bar or party didn't compare to him staying safe. Even after we had children, I reminded him. "I'll come get you, even if I have to bring the kids." All of our friends knew this rule, too.

My cheeks flushed with his admission. The last few weeks, we had been on civil terms but not necessarily speaking. Our family was leaving in a couple days for Disney World, a vacation my parents were gifting to us so we could spend time with my whole family. My fingers curled around the phone, knowing he could have made so many different choices along the way—decisions that would have avoided this situation.

When Chris finally arrived home, I couldn't make eye contact with him, my disappointment and anger fueling my inability to give him the respect eye contact offers. He tried to seem remorseful with empty apologies, but it seemed to me his regret was at being caught, not in the act of driving under the influence and costing our relationship and our family so much. I told him his usual gifts to appease the situation wouldn't work. He decided sex would solve our problem. From here forward, physical intimacy in bed became a tool he would wield in our relationship—"a way to release his inner demons," he would tell me. He even used this crass comment within our friendship circles, humiliating me. In hindsight, I understand he used this dominating and animalistic act to control me, as if sex equated to ownership and "I'm sorry" led to fetishes he picked up along the way, which he expected me to fulfill "as his wife."

During the trip to Disney, he and my parents became like oil and water. The DUI was part of it, but it had become more like the cherry on top in a long line of ways they could see he was not caring for our family. In the past, he had missed family holiday events and often treated people with curt disregard. I decided to focus on our girls while at Disney World, stuffing my rage just under the surface. I didn't fool anyone.

Chris had lost his driver's license for thirty days, forcing me to drive him everywhere with our infant, Madison, in tow, while also taking Savannah back and forth to preschool. And all while I was still breastfeeding. But the bigger picture was worse. We spent the next year dealing with court appointments, attorney fees, and drug and alcohol counseling, all of which we had to pay for out of pocket. Home life was a mess.

2001

I wish this brush with the law and subsequent family stress or Madison's birth had changed Chris. I think it made his drinking worse. Chris frequently left us home alone to hang out with friends, partying until early into the morning hours. He became paranoid, believing everyone was out to get him. My efforts to convince him he could hang out with friends without drinking went unheeded.

"Chris, you can have fun without getting drunk!"

He couldn't do that.

Early one morning, I received another phone call that woke me up from a deep sleep.

"If someone doesn't come pick up Chris, the police are going to arrest him."

At 10:45 the evening before, as I was heading to bed, Chris was assuring me he was sober. Obviously, he wasn't. A friend had called to warn me about his erratic behavior. He had tried to help Chris but ended up in a fight with him, and Chris had bitten him.

"He can't come home." The intensity of my anger surprised even me. I had never been so forceful. My hands shook. "I'm not dealing with him anymore."

My mom was at the house, staying with us, and she awoke to hear all this. I called Chris's brother and told him he should go pick him up but not to bring him to our house.

"Take his keys. Otherwise, he'll get in the car and drive off."

When they reached Chris, Chris called and was spewing hateful comments because I didn't want him coming home.

"You lazy, fat piece of . . .! You don't make any money! If you don't let me in when I get there, you can just pack your bags and get the 'f' out of *my* house!"

I hung up without responding and made sure the doors were locked, hoping Chris's brother would keep the house keys from Chris. My mom stood and watched with horror, taken aback by Chris's harsh words that echoed through the phone.

"I'm done with this nonsense!" I half cried, half yelled.

When Chris sobered up, he ran off. He called me that day, instituting a new threat: "I'm going to kill myself." I would later learn from him, it's the consummate manipulative threat. He wouldn't tell me where he was, so I called the police. When they arrived, I explained the situation, including his threats to end his life. The officers advised me to get a protective order against Chris.

So that weekend, with trepidation and a heavy heart, I went to the courthouse, and the judge issued an emergency restraining order and child abuse protective order, considering Chris a danger to the girls and me.

As is typical in abusive relationships, in the next couple of days, Chris ended up apologizing and begging me to let him return home. "I love you and the girls. I'll do anything."

I felt sadness and had compassion for him (not for myself), and I acquiesced. What I did for myself was write down everything I wanted from him to make our marriage work. I still have the list today.

No more drinking with friends.
Family must come first.
You have to go to counseling.
You have to go on a legitimate job search.

Throughout our marriage, Chris had chosen his friends over me. It stung. No spouse wants to be second or third fiddle, especially to alcohol and friends who aren't pointing each other in the right direction. Often, Chris would target me as the butt of his jokes in front of his friends, much like how his family picked on each other while he grew up. And at times, those jokes included private information that I did not want shared with others. He always followed his mean-spirited wisecracks with "I'm just joking," as if that made it all okay.

When Chris belittled me, the kids, and my education, I felt trapped and small, hating the words but hating the feelings those words caused even more. I was finishing my bachelor's degree, and was proud of how I was juggling the many plates Chris left me to handle on my own. I was hurt that Chris blamed me for a messy house, when it was all I could do to keep up with my evening class, schoolwork, the girls, our struggling finances, and his alcoholism.

He performed bathroom checks, inspecting the insides of the toilets as if we were part of the military, too. If he saw dirt or grime, we were "disgusting pigs," not worthy to be part of his family unit. I was very much the co-dependent spouse of an addict and a controlling husband. And while I didn't know to call it that at the time, I knew deep down, that I deserved better. But the knowing was deep enough that I didn't quite believe it throughout the daily angst.

Most of all, my heart ached when Chris acted as if I was different when he was the one who had changed. Our fun year of dating felt light years away, not just four years removed. Looking back, there was simply not enough time to get to really know each other before we were married and then became parents.

The girls and I felt like a burden to him. Chris continued to flee—both physically and emotionally—every time a situation came up that required his attention. Financial issues. Parenting decisions. Our relationship. They overwhelmed him, and he'd simply leave the house, driving away, leaving me wondering when he'd come back. It reminded me of the beach vacation with his family years before, when he walked out of the house and didn't return for hours.

Even with my list of "demands" to re-enter our home, Chris didn't change. Over the next couple of years, it seemed he had joined some sort of "speeding ticket of the month" club, racking up fees left and right.

His verbal tirades and physical abuse continued when he was home. He called me names and threw things, trying to hit me or the wall behind me. Then, the verbal abuse trickled down a generation, and Savannah became one of his targets. He'd yell at her for little things—behaviors that all kids do—such as spilling a drink. To him, her childlike actions and words were personal attacks.

At first, he was hard on Savannah. Then, he became rough with her when he wanted her to do things—and do them a certain way—and she wasn't able to meet his expectations. He was not a dad; he was a bully, grabbing her forcefully as he yelled at her. Per my requests and then later, more forceful demands, he wasn't allowed to spank her. I was afraid of what he might do to her. So when she didn't do her chores or her schoolwork or her routine activities the way he expected, he gave up on her. At least he stopped touching her.

2002

We couldn't keep up with the bills, Chris's tickets, and his partying expenses, and eventually, were forced to sell our house. Thankfully, friends of ours bought it, and we moved in with my parents in upstate New York.

In the beginning, Chris played the game. A pattern had emerged over the years. Chris was able to control his emotions, and I would assess our home life as fair. But about every six months or so, Chris would have enormous blow-ups, where it seemed all the stress or energy he used to control his outbursts would finally hit a head. I was on the receiving end of his yo-yo-like emotions. The result was scary. The blow-ups would last days, sometimes weeks at a time. Between them, I'd mistakenly believe things would be better, and I'd fall into optimism, only to be disappointed again.

There were only a few issues at my parents' house until one day, a monster-sized meltdown stormed through our family yet again. Chris assumed we were home alone in the basement of my parent's house, but my brother was a couple floors above us. Something happened—I don't remember what it was, but often, it was a stressful event, small argument, or a fictitious circumstance in Chris's mind that caused his cyclic eruptions. Chris roared at me, and he slammed a door in my face. My hand was caught between the door and the frame, which caused me to let out a loud scream. In return, Chris's rage intensified, blaming me for having my hand where it didn't belong. My brother heard the commotion and came racing down the stairs.

It was always interesting to me that Chris could portray such a different personality when confronted by other people. As soon as my brother entered the scene, Chris pulled his mask back on.

"I'm so sorry. It was an accident. I didn't see her hand." Chris told my brother. For reasons unknown, Chris was fearful of my brother, even though my brother was shorter than him. For the second time, someone else intervened, ending Chris's rampage.

Soon after, Chris spiraled, claiming he "hated the world and everyone in it." His paranoia re-emerged, causing him to believe everyone was out to get him. He told me he couldn't live with my family anymore and gave me an ultimatum.

"I don't care if you come with me or not, but I'm leaving," he told me one day in front of my parents. At this point, he didn't care who witnessed his erratic behavior. After years of giving quiet support and offering me a place to stay if I needed somewhere to run, my parents had seen enough. Their indirect support turned into loud pleas.

"Lara, you don't have to go with him. We can help you. You and the girls will be okay. Let him leave," they begged me. My heart burst wide open, torn between the family who supported me and the husband who I had to constantly prove something to. I loved them all.

As with many spouses in my predicament, I worried about how I'd make ends meet. I was afraid of the unknown, and I had become so wrapped up in our relationship that I couldn't picture our family falling apart. And I felt I would be letting Chris down again if I left him. I had promised to love Chris when we were married. I wasn't ready to admit that the abuse warranted a new life just yet. I had learned to trust one of the lies Chris had planted in my mind over the years. The belief that no one else would want me fueled my reluctance to stay behind with my parents and start over. Deep down, in places women can't usually acknowledge when they're under the control of an abuser, I wondered if everyone else saw me as a fat, lazy woman, even though I was sure, somewhere in the pit of my soul, that I wasn't.

So I called Chris and begged him to return to the house and take us back.

"Please don't leave. Whatever we need to do, let's do it. I'm so sorry. Whatever you want . . ."

––––––––––––

Words are powerful, but they aren't magical. The reasons spouses stay in abusive relationships are complex. Societal barriers are an important part of this story. We live in a society that understands and expounds the difficulties associated with single parenting. As young girls, we are taught to find the happy ever after. When we believe we have, it's hard to let it go, even in spite of the way our spouses make us feel in abusive relationships. We're taught to believe our identities and feelings of self-worth are tied to our ability to get married . . . and stay married.

I was still in school, had already given up a career in finance, and now had two daughters depending on what I hoped could be a stable and secure family unit. Even though my parents had offered to help us, my independent nature and limiting beliefs about my worth condemned my current situation, shaming me and fueling a fear that I wouldn't be able to support us.

Hope is our greatest asset, but it can also be our greatest obstacle. It depends on what, or who, we put our hope in. In my case, I hoped Chris would change. I hoped I could make this marriage viable if I tried harder, even gave in a bit more. I hoped for a miracle, and I was content to stick around and keep striving for an ending I knew, in the end, was unlikely.

When I watched Chris drive away, I did what I often had done over the years. I rationalized his behavior away, telling myself it was caused by stress, alcohol, living with my family and being far from his own, employment instability, and more. His abuse was inconsistent, so it was easy to compartmentalize his erratic actions. During those times he wasn't blowing up, I told myself he was still a good person. He just had to "let off steam."

CHAPTER 5

THE TALE OF TWO VACATIONS

"The one thing that doesn't abide by majority rule is a person's conscience."
—**Harper Lee** in *To Kill a Mockingbird*

W hen I told Chris I'd do anything to keep the family together, he made the decision we would move back to the Lehigh Valley area in Pennsylvania. I relented. Chris used our daughter's inheritance checks from their great grandparents to hire movers to help, and his parents found us a townhome rental, sight unseen on our end, located five minutes from their house.

Anxiety and fear crept back into my life. Over the years, I had noticed the closer Chris was to his family, the more violent he became under our own roof. This would be no exception.

The townhome was tiny. And Chris became a larger-than-life monster in the privacy of our home, a place with few places to hide. When triggered, Chris would kick holes in the walls. The girls and I cowered. On one occasion, Chris became so enraged when I had accidently let water spill over our kitchen sink and onto the floor that I had to call his parents. He had gone on a rampage, kicking the couches in our living room until his foot created gaping holes in the fabric. He wouldn't stop, so I grabbed our kids and fled to his brother's house, while his parents sped over to our townhouse to calm him down.

After this event, nothing was ever discussed between us or his family. It was swept under the rug, as had so many other things. His parents had been privy to it all: the DUI, the protective order . . . all of it. Years earlier, Chris's dad, Henry, had sat him down and begged him to "get it together." I sat nearby, listening with the weight of embarrassment, both for Chris and me.

2004

Chris applied to the Navy Exchange System—the on-base shopping centers for the Navy—and found a job that took him on a long commute to Philadelphia every day. I had found work at a local learning center based in a church. Loving my job, having a sense of community among my coworkers, and having Chris out of the house for many hours at a time created a long-awaited sense of peace. I could bring Madison to work with me since she was enrolled in the church's preschool, and Savannah joined us after school. I thrived at work with my children close to me. It provided me with the energy I needed to ignore our home life when Chris returned from work each day.

It seems strange that we need energy to ignore things. But it's true. Bullies. Abusive spouses. Dysfunctional relationships. Individuals who have no boundaries. These types of people steal energy through manipulation and intimidation.

This is the year we went on vacation with Chris's family. Everyone was there, including his sister and her husband. I was wary, on high alert. Honestly, wary is too nice a word. I despised having to go. I didn't want to spend so much of our money spending time with his sister, Aline, and her husband. Chris was reluctant, as well.

It was a crappy vacation, but in hindsight, it was meaningful to me in that it was the last one we'd have with Henry. Aline and I ended up in a huge argument, much to the entertainment of the rest of the family. I regret going toe-to-toe with someone so immature and disrespectful. I should have done better and remained calm, ignoring her like everyone else did, as she bossed family members around.

I promised this wouldn't be a one-sided, tell-all book. For me, it's important that people understand Chris didn't like his sister, either. It wasn't just a sibling rivalry. He didn't trust her and wanted no contact with her.

I had been battling migraines since the age of eleven. I carried potent medication with me that had to be timed and regulated by someone other than me when I took it. During the vacation, a migraine enveloped my body, and even though Chris had told me not to bring it out, I had to take my medication. Chris was afraid his sister's husband would take it—not to cause me more pain but for other reasons we suspected.

A few days in, some of my migraine medicine went missing. Later, while on speaker phone with me standing next to him, Chris commented to his mother about the disappearance. "Maybe your daughter took it," she replied, referring to our eight-year-old. The idea was ludicrous. If that were true, and either of my girls had ingested a whole bottle of these pills, we would have needed to rush them to the hospital. His mom called us liars, never willing to admit alternative reasons that may have included her own daughter's husband, a known drug addict, and I vowed never to vacation with Aline and her husband again. Feeling as offended as me, Chris agreed. I felt affirmed by Chris's anger. It felt like finally, we were on the same page about something.

This was the year I finally graduated with my bachelor's degree after years of attending school part-time. Elated, my parents planned a graduation party. Chris's family refused to attend. It was their way of punishing me for refusing to apologize to Aline for the argument we had while on vacation.

During the Tur Family vacation, Henry had seemed distant. Looking back, I believe he was already feeling unwell. A few months after the trip, he was diagnosed with terminal colon cancer. As Christmas approached, Chris's family asked everyone to be close and spend the holiday with Chris's dad, as we suspected his time was near. I struggled on many levels.

I adored Henry. His kindness toward me and the girls never went unappreciated. Despite stories and rumors of his abuse toward Chris's mom, I never saw it nor experienced it. He and I had enjoyed a good relationship, one filled with mutual regard. I also wanted to spend time with Chris's grandmother, Henry's mom. She was a gem, always so good to our kids. I carried a truck load of respect for both of these individuals.

However, I didn't want to see the rest of Chris's family. His mom had blamed me for the vacation-time argument with his sister and their retributive graduation party absence had left me feeling sour. The idea that my behavior offended her but her daughter's didn't left me confused and feeling the weight of a thousand injustices. There was a lot of tension, and the stress of the family dynamics was always so much to bear. In the end, I couldn't *not* go spend Christmas at their house. Henry meant too much to me, so I pushed through. And I'm glad I did. The holiday passed by, and Chris's dad hung on.

2005

Shortly after starting work at the church-based learning center, I started to attend church there on Sundays. I brought Madison and Savannah with me, and we went faithfully, even when Chris declined—which was often. The routine and the people there made space for peace and calm in my chaotic life.

In the summer of 2005, we embarked on another Disney vacation with my family. I hoped and prayed it would be care-free, that Chris would be in control of his outbursts, and we could finally enjoy a vacation together as a family. My hopes materialized.

The girls were old enough to be enamored with everything Disney, and it was a magical time away. Madison had discovered a deep fondness—more like an obsession—with all things Cinderella. She ate, slept, and breathed Cinderella, and we loved watching her delight in the princess. She even went home with the authentic Cinderella wedding dress.

Chris had a great time, too. Sure there were little bumps along the way, but I think Chris and I were able to catch a glimpse of the reasons we fell in love in the first place. The vacation was absolutely wonderful.

When we returned from Disney, Henry took a turn for the worse. It was clear we would need to focus on his remaining days as he struggled with his health. It was a tough time as everyone's memories of the Tur family vacation resurfaced, and the sadness of losing the patriarch of the Tur family flooded all of our hearts.

Chris's sister and her husband were strangely absent for much of the time. No one had any complaints. Chris's mother was grieving the loss of Henry in her own way. She voiced her confusion about why her sons were doting on him on his deathbed when Henry was never there for them while they were growing up. I can't imagine the depth of sorrow caused by watching your spouse of so many years fighting for a life that can't be saved, so I held compassion for her. Ann and I actually grew closer during this time as she shared some not-so-pleasant sides of her marriage with Henry. I could identify with the silent suffering of another wife.

We rotated visits with Chris's brothers, all of us retreating to our respective homes to grab showers and a change of clothes in shifts. Chris's sister and her husband fluttered in and out on occasion in the final days. At one point, some of Henry's pain medication for the chemotherapy treatments went missing. Chris and I could only shake our heads.

The most heartbreaking event was when Aline started an unabashedly selfish argument on the front lawn of the Tur home. It was a fight over money. Henry hadn't passed yet, and she was demanding the money she deserved from his estate. I grabbed all the children and headed to the basement so they wouldn't hear the commotion. Chris, his siblings, and their spouses all stayed on the lawn. It was the ugliest family dispute I had witnessed thus far. I am sure everyone's emotions were running at a thousand percent with the grief that had set in, but it was still inappropriate. I mention this event to provide context for my own story—the one that others have reshaped over the years, pegging me as an enemy. Nearly every Tur family member wrestled (wrestles) with money and other financial strongholds.

When Henry succumbed to his cancer, we were all bedside, with the exception of Aline and her husband. I felt honored to write Henry's obituary because he had been such a kind and good man to me. Though, given my last conversations with Ann, I was reminded that how people see families from the outside can be so vastly different from the truth of what is happening under the roof and between the walls.

––––––––––

A year passed, and the Turs were still fighting over family money. The email strings revealed the nasty relationship Aline had with most of the other family members. In one, she told everyone we were dead to her, and at that point, Chris shared with me he would never speak to her again. It was so ugly that the girls and I were never allowed to mention her name in our home. She became known as Voldemort—or the person who shall never be named—from the *Harry Potter* series. Madison and Savannah had effectively lost an aunt, though I wasn't the least bit sad about it. From my experience, she hadn't been a good role model, not even a respectable person. Chris had one final encounter with his sister at another funeral, and when he returned, he said the experience solidified his decision to keep her out of our lives.

After Henry's death, we moved to Pax River, the Naval Air Station at Patuxent River in Maryland, and Chris's career with the Navy Exchange took off.

CHAPTER 6

BROKEN BONES

"Waste no more time arguing about what a good man should be. Be one."

—Marcus Aurelius

M oving around, sometimes every other year, became our modus operandi. At times, I was not part of the decision to relocate. This particular move was all Chris's idea, as he had received a promotion of sorts at the Navy Exchange, which meant a little more money than before. So one day, he informed us we were moving, and I was expected to drop the job I had and support his desire to relocate again. I didn't put up much of an argument because I knew bases were closing, and this move would mean more job security for Chris. Though, I battled disappointment because I had been up for a promotion at the learning center. My mechanical, routine existence wore on me. On one level, I suspected part of his desire to move was to further distance himself from his family and the drama they continued to create. We were still copied on email strings between his mom and sister about unpaid bills and other things we didn't care to follow.

At Pax River, we rented a beautiful home on the Potomac River. Chris and I weren't close at this point. Our marriage was one of logistics. His violent and erratic mood swings and cyclic outbursts had continued through the years, and I was hopeful this continued distancing from his family would help quiet his rageful events. It seemed no one was getting along.

In Maryland, the base was great, but we didn't quite get settled into the area. I had started on my master's degree and found a job working with young adults, teaching life skills, which I loved. However, we both felt lonely, and after eighteen months, we were packing up our things again in July of 2007. The schools weren't fantastic, so we moved to Virginia Beach, where Chris accepted another job within the Navy Exchange and where Savannah, who was now in middle school, could receive better educational opportunities.

Chris continued to distance himself from childhood friends and family, even as I craved social interaction, wanting to combat the loneliness that covered me from head to toe. He didn't tell any of his old friends we had moved again. One guy paid a website-based service to find us. Chris ranted about an invasion of privacy. "If I wanted people to know where we are, I'd tell them!"

This time, we rented a five-bedroom home, which gave Chris and me plenty of space to continue living somewhat separate lives. With the distance we had put between ourselves and the Tur family, Chris seemed to mellow out a bit. We only saw them at holidays, and it just wasn't the same without Henry. Chris became absorbed in his work, his superiors even recommended him for an executive leadership training program.

At home, even though there was intermittent peace, I was tasked with carrying the full burden of the family, the finances, the large house, the girls' growing schedules, my schooling, and any part-time or flex-time job I could find. I finished my master's degree and was moving on to a Ph.D. program. My life was chaotic. Perhaps, it was by choice. The busier I was, the less time I had to reflect on our distant marriage.

Our financial picture didn't change much with this move. Chris, again without consulting me as his wife, traded in his car and purchased a sports car that I couldn't use since I didn't know how to drive a standard transmission. His speeding tickets piled up again. Then, just when I thought his behavior had mellowed, he started staying out late again. Even though the Navy Exchange was not open twenty-four hours, he often didn't come home until 3:00 a.m., citing work reasons. I didn't believe him. When I called him out on the lies, he would tell me I was crazy. I've since learned there is a term for this phenomenon. It's called the "crazy-maker effect," where addicts turn the tables and lay blame on those around them.

I continued my schooling and worked two jobs to help make ends meet—counseling and teaching at a local college. Living paycheck to paycheck didn't help our relationship. Eventually, I had to quit counseling because it wasn't conducive to the needs of our family. Chris wasn't willing to help out with the girls or house. It was the second time in our marriage when his lack of support and spending frenzies forced me to cut back on my career opportunities.

Savannah started high school, and people often referred to her and Madison as our mini-mes. Savannah looked so much like Chris, and her personality often mirrored his. They sported dark features, piercing brown eyes and hair to match. Though stubborn, like two mules bargaining with their handlers, both Chris and Savannah harbored sensitivity, too. Savannah, like Chris, had the ability to enter any room and give people the impression of confidence, even though she sheltered fragility and self-doubt. People gravitated to Savannah. And both had a vicious bite when cornered, questioned, or feeling disrespected. On the flip side, both had hearts that leaned toward helping others in distress. Their motives, however, differed.

Madison takes after me. In a line of eight children in her generation on the Tur side, she was the only fair-skinned, blonde child. She looked like the original Gerber baby, complete with light eyes beneath prominent lashes. This had garnered much attention from Henry who had been born in Cuba. Madison has always been outspoken, independent, and able to articulate her opinion. She was (and is) my budding attorney.

Both girls are intelligent and able to argue their points to exhaustion. As Savannah grew older, she and Chris tangled with each other. She had always been athletic—a natural—and in some ways, I think he tried to turn her into the boy he never had. At the very least, he was living vicariously through her. He coached as many of her sports teams as he could. Chris wanted to be connected, but he also wanted to be the best. His focus on appearances, labels, and other external validation came through in the way he interacted with Savannah. They butted heads frequently. Often, he forced both girls to participate in sports he thought were appropriate, not the ones they wanted to try. Since Virginia Beach didn't have hockey, he pushed Savannah to play lacrosse, and she eventually relented.

From the outside looking in, others likely saw passion. Some saw the obsession. We felt it. Savannah could never miss a practice. It was go-go-go, even when she was exhausted or busy with school responsibilities. Both girls wanted to please Chris, and being number one in whatever they were doing meant earning his respect and praise. Eventually, with maturity, Savannah started participating in other sports, which he wasn't involved with, but he'd be there on the sidelines and unofficially coach her from there.

One day, they became engaged in a heated argument. The topic is not relevant. In my opinion, most of their arguments were meaningless battles between two strong-willed people. Chris liked to have an uber organized house. It was another way he controlled us. When he claimed it was a cleaning day, we all had to clean. The expectation was that we put down everything else we wanted to do and join him.

For example, the girls had to clean their rooms to a ridiculous level, and if they didn't straighten up and organize to his satisfaction, he exploded. We called it "building Mount Suribachi," which is a small, dormant volcano on Iwo Jima in Japan. It was the site where U.S. Marines raised a flag in 1945, the photo becoming a well-known World War II memory. If Madison and Savannah's dresser drawers weren't organized to his satisfaction, he would yank them out and dump them in the middle of their rooms, demanding they start from scratch and creating this mountain of stuff and a lot of hurt feelings.

To avoid this, I would often go ahead of him and beg the girls to do a good job so we could all avoid Chris's outbursts. I just couldn't take listening to Chris yell and the girls cry. Looking back, I realize this enabled his behavior, and I hope my girls know none of this was their fault.

Back to this particular day, the family was cleaning out the garage, and Chris was getting on Savannah about something. He asked her to put the vacuum pieces back together, and instead, she laid them on a step leading into the house. "Do it yourself," she said with defiance. I was inside, listening to their spat, and when I walked back out, I slipped on the steps where the vacuum pieces lay and broke my foot.

Chris was very good at what I call the "Nightingale" thing. All the right buttons were pushed when he could swoop in to save the day.

This day was no different. He picked me up, sped off to the emergency room, and then proceeded to tell anyone and everyone how he rescued me and was taking care of me while I journeyed through multiple surgeries and rehabilitation in the coming months and years. In reality, my parents and my best friend took care of the majority of my needs and the girls' needs while Chris worked. It's not like he could quit his job. I didn't expect him to. I also didn't expect him to create this story about how he was doing everything from caring for me to cooking to cleaning the house and parenting our children. It just wasn't true.

Chris wanted all stories in life to go like this: Chris sees a problem. Chris fixes the problem (or tries to). Chris receives accolades and praise. I know this sounds petty and harsh. Trust me. But I also know that emotionally healthy people want the story of life to go something like this: We are born. We go through stuff. We learn. We feel empowered. We become individuals who help each other as we pursue our own interests and solve problems. We all find happiness as we pursue our individual gifts, talents, and purposes. Chris never wanted me to feel empowered. He didn't want me to problem solve or give advice. Rather, he wanted all glory for himself. He wanted me dependent on him.

Over the years, we had mastered the public perception and played "the game," convincing many around us we shared a good marriage. And as Chris perfected the art of donning and removing his mask, I often dismissed the magnitude of the abuse that occurred behind closed doors. As my friends and family spent more time at our house, helping with cooking and cleaning while I mended from my broken foot, Chris's mask started to slip off, allowing others to catch more and more glimpses of the true person that was Chris Tur. His short-tempered and mean-spirited jabs at me both startled and concerned my family and friends.

My aunt was the next to witness Chris's "behind closed doors" persona—the verbal abuse, in particular. At my brother's wedding in Maine, she walked in on one of his belittling attacks as we hid away in a room. Chris was lecturing me about something, and when she entered, she attempted to ease herself back out of the door into the hall, clearly startled by the harsh tone Chris was using. Within a tenth of a second, Chris noticed her, turned around, immediately slapped a smile on his face, and pleasantly engaged her as if what she had just heard never happened.

As best man, Chris moved through the ceremony with what I viewed as an elaborate display of showmanship. His toast was exceptional, moving and emotional—a wonderful gift for my brother and his new wife. However, I sat there knowing that every word carried the stench of lies.

On the drive home from the wedding—a long ride from Maine to Virginia—our girls bickered in the car. The typical "this is my space" fighting, which all kids master by age four. It's something every parent faces, but that doesn't make it any less annoying. I asked the girls to stop several times. After a few more miles of "Why are you breathing my air?" battles, Chris couldn't take it any longer.

Growing up, Chris's parents believed in gaining "respect" and control by spanking their children as a form of discipline. It was the opposite philosophy in my family. My parents were not physical discipliners, and I often counseled other families to find more creative ways to dish out consequences. I have never thought spanking should be a first or second strategy but rather a last resort when all the other parenting tools have been exhausted. Over the years of my educational journey and counseling experience, I saw how physical discipline leaves everyone feeling defeated in the end. Even though Chris did not agree with me on this, our kids had never been spanked.

In that car on that long journey down the East Coast, we were all feeling a bit crazy, itching to get out of the car. So when the girls continued to bicker, Chris lost it. Instead of pulling over to let everyone get some air or have a talk with the girls, as he's speeding down the interstate, he reaches around and tries to punch Savannah who was sitting behind him. The girls and I screamed. Savannah, thankfully, pulled her legs up as she shrank back into the unforgiving seatback to block Chris's fist. His balled-up hand met her knee, and the force of his punch broke his hand. It swelled immediately.

Chris continued driving as the girls and I remained silent and still, fearful that any movement or sound might lead to more violence. I had never felt so helpless. As a mom who wanted nothing more than to protect her girls, I felt caged in that car, a victim of both Chris's violence and the speeding vehicle from which we couldn't escape.

Chris became outraged as the pain traveled through his arm. Finally, he stopped to get a bag of ice. Savannah was terrified, feeling both relief it wasn't her face or stomach, but also worried Chris would blame her for his pain. Chris remained focused on his throbbing hand, and I sat in the passenger seat, my insides set on a low boil, maintaining my emotions so as not to create another issue in the small confines of the car. As I sat, frozen, a part of me died.

When we arrived home, Chris visited the same doctor I had seen for my broken foot.

"What happened?" the orthopedist asked.

"We were stuck in traffic coming home from Maine. I got frustrated and punched the gearshift."

The story was believable, still an angry action born from Chris's emotional overload, which people closest to him grew to expect from him. "That's just Chris." The girls and I never corrected his story. We simply let it go, praying it wouldn't happen again. His fractured hand was casted, and he was told to leave it alone for six weeks.

After a few weeks, maybe three, my girlfriend, Amy, visited. We were standing in the kitchen when Chris got home from work; he was worked up and irritable. He'd had enough of the cast. Calling the doctor, Chris became angrier when the medical staff told him and they wouldn't remove his cast early. It was a liability for them. He must allow enough time for his hand to heal, or it could easily fracture again.

Chris didn't hang up the phone, he threw it. Going berserk, he said, "I'll just saw the (explicative) thing off." My friend and I pleaded with him to calm down. His irrationality scared us and the girls, who were home, listening to the whole thing.

"Chris, just do your time," I said.

"No! It's my hand. I can do what I want!"

He went to his tool bench and grabbed a saw. Then, he proceeded to cut the cast off. I was terrified he was going to cut his arm. During the whole event, he screamed: "Leave me the [f] alone!"

When he finished, he left, driving away like a mad man.

Amy stared at me in disbelief.

We moved back into the kitchen. "There's something going on with him," I confided in a whisper. "We've been dealing with these cycles of violence and craziness for a while." It was the first time she had witnessed his impulsivity and hyper-emotional behavior and the first time I admitted to someone I had a problem. I assumed Chris was cheating on me. It was easy to reach that sort of conclusion with the late nights, the lack of intimacy between us, and his growing temper and impatience toward the girls and me, as if he resented our existence.

What I didn't share with Amy was that Chris had complete control over me. I didn't let her fully into our nightmare nor did I describe the level of abuse I encountered. Honestly, I'm not sure I realized the extent of it or its impact on me at the time. It's easy to look back or judge someone else's experience, but it's quite another thing to admit your own victimization.

And I was certainly being victimized. I never enjoyed a stable job to call my own over the years. With every quick move, any job equity I had built up vanished, just like our whereabouts. We had married with joint accounts, and when he didn't pay bills, my credit was ruined. Then, he had transferred everything to his name, so I couldn't even build credit on my own. Trapped, with nothing to call my own—a house, a career, or even my identity—I felt left with little choices. And when we lose the ability to see our choices, depression sets in.

CHAPTER 7

GTMO

"The truly scary thing about undiscovered lies is that they have a greater capacity to diminish us than exposed ones. They erode our strength, our self-esteem, our very foundation."
—Cheryl Hughes

Early Winter 2010

T he scene had been set for me to jump on board when Chris explained to me there was a possible overseas opportunity for him, and he wanted to move again. He laid out his case bare: higher pay, no mortgage or rent while living on the base, a lower cost of living, and no need to pay for utilities.

Our family was broken, and I felt numb. After fifteen years of marriage, Chris's multiple DUIs and tickets, nearly losing our first home in foreclosure, on and off marriage counseling, Chris's bouts in drug and alcohol counseling, a season spent on welfare, multiple job changes and moves, and my battles with loneliness, depression, and fear, it was easy for me to relent within minutes. Not only did I agree we could move overseas, I embraced the idea. I clung to the notion that a fresh start in a different country would mean a completely new start in our relationship. Could I find the man I had fallen in love with in 1995? Could we be happy? I realize now this type of thinking highlighted my own mental health issues.

In short order, both Chris and I were running away from the life we had been living. He from his inner demons, his family's drama, and his cyclic anger. Me from the abuse at his hands and lips, the idea I was failing myself and my daughters, the belief I was wasting my hard-earned education, and the numbness of feeling trapped in a life I never envisioned for myself when, as a little girl, I had looked ahead with joyful anticipation to adulthood.

In 2011, the opportunity materialized. It was real. Naval Station Guantanamo Bay (NSGB), otherwise known as GTMO—pronounced "Gitmo" because of the way the first U.S. military inhabitants at the base said it—is the oldest overseas U.S. Naval Base and sits on the southeastern end of Cuba in the Caribbean Sea. I started planning and packing immediately.

My excitement about starting over fueled me, giving me energy I had been missing over the previous decade as my identity had been stripped away, layer by layer. I don't think I'm alone in the thought that if we can pick up, move somewhere far away, maybe even change our names, we can start over and live a different life. New beginnings motivate many of us. They are opportunities to reframe ourselves, painting a new picture of who we are, maybe discovering who we are meant to be.

I was ready. I researched the base and Cuba in general, discovering numerous facts and details ahead of our move.

Guantanamo Bay Naval Station houses 6,500–8,000 from the U.S. Navy, Marines, Army, Coast Guard, government employees, contractors, and their dependent families, but forty percent of the base is populated by migrant workers, hired as civilian contractors for the military— foreign nationals from Jamaica and the Philippines. It is the only U.S. military base located in a communist country. The base is separated into the Naval base side, where we would live, and the JTF, or Joint Task Force, side. The JTF side is where the detainees are housed.

Just ahead of our arrival, the biggest news coming out of GTMO was the presidential executive orders, coming from President Obama, directing the CIA to shut its remaining network of secret prisons based there, those made infamous in 2004 when prisoner abuse and torture came to the public's attention with the publication of certain photos by *CBS* News. However, Obama backpedaled and not long after, issued orders that permitted ongoing detention of prisoners, which continues to this day.

My main focus was the newness of an overseas base. It wouldn't have mattered where we headed, my thoughts had landed and buried themselves deep into the idea of starting over. I discovered—through a friend who worked at DoDEA, the Department of Defense Education Activity—that the schools were good at this base. I felt relief for my girls. Hope bloomed, and my constant self-talk, now filled with optimism, said, "Maybe this will all work out."

Madison was still young and ready for anything. Entering middle school, she didn't have many close ties to our current life. Her life could be summed up like most other tweens—self-discovery. Savannah, on the other hand, was involved in multiple sports programs and was halfway through high school. She and her friends were tight, and her extra-curricular activities meant everything to her.

I knew how she would receive the news because I, too, had moved 3,000 miles across the country in the middle of high school. I understood the loss, but at the same time, I believed our decision would help the greater good—the whole family. I considered everyone's physical, mental, and emotional health and wellbeing. GTMO would be good for us.

On Valentine's Day, 2011, we went out to dinner as a family. Chris and I announced our decision to move overseas to our girls.

"We're going to Guantanamo Bay Naval Station . . . in Cuba."

From that point, everything moved quickly. We told our families, and I quit my job. My parents were thrilled with the exciting opportunity but sad to see me and the girls move so far away. Other family members were less than happy for us, making it seem as if we were moving to the Congo. They told us they wouldn't visit, no matter how beautiful we told them Cuba was rumored to be.

Chris sold his sports car since we were only permitted one car on the island. Excitement was building, and though Savannah was the least happy of all of us, we knew over time, she would be able to reconcile the idea of moving to Cuba.

Chris moved down ahead of us as he secured housing, and I stayed back to support the girls' transition. They finished out school, and the three of us traveled a bit, taking our time to say good-bye to friends and family. We visited New York City, spent time traveling with my parents in their RV, briefly visited with my brother and his family and Chris's brothers and mom, and then made our way back to Virginia Beach, so I could finalize medical records and conquer the other odds and ends associated with an international move.

The day came for our military flight to Jacksonville and then on to GTMO. The three of us felt anticipation surging through our bodies, and my heart was beating to the rhythm those who embark on big adventures know well. I wondered if I had just put all my eggs in one glorious Caribbean basket. Even our dog, who traveled with us, was excited, and everything went smoothly.

When we touched down in Guantanamo Bay, the first thing the crew did was hand us water bottles and encourage us to stay hydrated. Our bodies were not used to the hot and salty air, and after the flight, they said we would need the extra fluids. I had lived in South Florida, California, and Virginia Beach, but nothing compared. It was truly beautiful.

True to their word, I became dehydrated, despite my compliance with drinking water, regular and flavored, and avoiding caffeine all day, and I found myself flat on my back hours later with a migraine.

Once I could move again, Chris gave me a tour of our cute, tropically-inspired block home, complete with bold colors, open air door and window units, and one bath. I stared in disbelief, biting my tongue as we squeezed into the tiny bathroom. I wanted things to go well. My hope outweighed my knowledge that at some point, a "one-butt" bathroom was not going to work with three females and a male who spent just as much time grooming and admiring himself in the mirror as we did. "We'll make it work," I said. In the spirit of all things new, I choked down my concerns and continued on the tour, making a note to buy floor-length mirrors for each bedroom.

The house was all at once beautiful and quaint. The temporary furniture appeared to be from the 1950s, and while never updated or changed out for a more modern look, it was all lovely. As I sat on the sofa, covered in a polyester blend fabric, I felt I had stepped back in time. The neighboring houses that lined the street reflected ours but in an array of pastel colors. Some blue. Others light green. And a few tan-colored homes, too. The smell of mangoes, papaya, and guava fruit permeated the outdoor space.

The area the base people inhabit is small, roughly five to ten square miles, even though the base is forty-five square miles in its entirety. There wasn't much sightseeing to be had, so we became familiar with the area quickly. Not only were there plenty of tarantulas, but there were land crab migrations that often stopped traffic as hundreds of these creatures crossed the roads. Thankfully, this migration was a seasonal phenomenon.

I was grateful we arrived in summertime. It meant Madison, Savannah, and I weren't the only people transitioning to the base for the first time. Families were coming and going with new orders, so we didn't feel so out of place as the "new kids" on the block. I helped them get involved with programs and fun activities, so they could meet other teens and tweens who were just arriving and avoid making close connections with kids who might be leaving the island soon. Savannah struggled a bit with the move, but I knew in time, with the positive vibe of the base, she would get through it.

Those who had lived there for any length of time were welcoming. We became quickly immersed in the lifestyle of the base. As part of the charm and "stepping back in time" culture, only a few people carried cell phones, and I was not one of them. Every place was deemed safe, from the stores to the recreation centers. Unlike in any place we had ever lived before, I felt comfortable sending my girls off on the busses that took them to the library or to other parts of the "little town."

Everyone knew everyone else, and I don't just mean knew names and faces. We realized within weeks that everyone at GTMO ate, slept, and breathed each other. It was part of the lax environment, a place where people knew from where you had come, what you did for work, who your kids were, and what time you went to bed. It's not like the friendships and relationships with coworkers or neighbors we build in the States. In Guantanamo Bay, every relationship is built quickly and intimately, and connections that traditionally take a lifetime to create are forged within a few short weeks or months. If you felt blue, there were twelve people ready to step in, either to lend a shoulder, make you smile, or offer a listening ear or advice. These are the types of relationships that never leave you, even when you leave the island behind.

Speaking of leaving the island: it is a popular base. Only a few want to leave. The military limits government employees, or GS, to five-year terms at GTMO, but it wasn't uncommon for officers and servicemen and servicewomen to withdraw to the States for the mandatory two years only to make their way back for another half decade at GTMO. Civilian contractors have no time limits, and many live on base for fifteen to twenty years, including those contractors from the Philippines, Jamaica, and even Cuba.

My life had changed. From living paycheck to paycheck to now able to afford a weekly in-house cleaning service and massages. I appreciated it all, never forgetting from where we had come, feeling financially stuck just a few short months before. The stress seemed to melt away. We embraced the military base, the people, and the culture. However, there was one aspect of life on base that caught me off guard and left me a tad uncomfortable, at first.

People don't like to talk about it, but GTMO had a lax drinking policy. Drinking alcohol was as prevalent as waking up to a sunny day, meaning it occurred every day. Backyard barbeques prevailed, and you could always find a place to sit in a lawn chair, share a few with a friend, and then drive home. There were no DUI checkpoints, no ride shares, and no taxi service. Even the CO, or commanding officer, in charge when we arrived communicated no policies or restrictions regarding alcohol consumption. This reinforced excessive drinking. This never sat well with me, not when I had years of living with someone who succumbed to alcohol under my belt.

While the kids enjoyed a new level of independence in this environment, after a certain time of day, I did not allow them to take the bus or walk home. I knew there were countless people on the roads who had ingested far more alcohol than any driver should. Without the risk of DUIs, I feared my kids' involvement in an accident. Our friends allowed their kids out later, but I did not.

Chris and I, for the most part, enjoyed the social aspects of the culture, meeting people through his work. After years of isolation and living with his growing disinterest in making or keeping friendships, the lifestyle at GTMO offered fresh air to our relationship and his psyche. We were finally making friends again. For the first time since our dating years, things were a bit peaceful, and we were having a good time. Life was fun and light-hearted but also serious. It was a military base, after all.

———————

Late Fall 2011

After a few months, I realized I had to make more use of my time and my education. Growing bored during the day, I decided to apply for jobs on base. I knew I could find something where I might utilize the various skills I had learned over the years. A position opened at the Fleet and Family Support Center for an education service facilitator. I was more than qualified with my counseling and teaching experience. I had even worked with GED students, military families, and was familiar with the G.I. Bill. It was not a far-fetched notion that I could fit the bill for this role. I interviewed and was offered the position. I started my new government position in January 2012.

Chris saw my position as a great publicity opportunity with the added benefit of financial gain. Soon after the offer, we attended a friend's birthday party. Chris stood up, interrupted conversation, and made a loud announcement that I had received a GS position. His over-the-top gesture appeared genuine to others, but deep down, I believed it was more about him than me. "What a supportive husband," people cooed. What they didn't know—and he did—was that I loathed public displays, especially ones that positioned me in any kind of spotlight. My mind skipped back to his marriage proposal in the restaurant a decade and a half before. The pit in my stomach warned me the "old" Chris was back.

My assumption was confirmed when later, he told me my degree was useless and the field in which I worked a joke. Publicly, he was the doting husband. Privately, he continued his belittling shots, never interested in what I was doing and rarely joining me for work-related events. My hope of rediscovering the man I thought I had married began its descent into oblivion.

The people I worked with were incredible, and we developed close friendships. Again, it's not like in the States where work is the boundary line, and once the day is over, you see your work friends again the next morning as you move into your separate lives for the evening hours. Work was home and home was work; nothing was siloed or compartmentalized at GTMO. The base, at this time, held 6,000 people. Most people assume GTMO is one large base, and we live among the Joint Task Force employees and are close to the camps that house detainees. That's an incorrect assumption. We lived on the Naval base side of a clearly separated and siloed area, and we didn't have access to visit, nor even view, anything that happened near the detention centers.

However, when I started this new role, I was tasked with facilitating classes for everyone at GTMO, working with the Joint Task Force, as well. The people in my classes included foreign nationals, GS and their families, military contractors and their families, and people from the school system. Not only was I humbled to have access to certain parts of the Joint Task Force areas—places we had only heard about on the news—the significance of my work empowered me. I made contacts and connections with a broad range of people daily.

The world I had just stepped into thrilled me after spending so many years believing I wasn't important or that I didn't matter. These were limiting lies formed from the verbal and emotional maltreatment I had endured, and this job was chipping away at them.

The other exciting aspect of my new job was having a hand in building curriculum and adjusting curriculum to meet the needs of the people I served. It took a lot of work, but for the first time, that work was meaningful to me, and my identity was coming into focus. I had loved all my previous jobs in the States, but I had never had permanency like this. It was a forty-hour per week role, and I loved every minute of those hours. The girls were old enough to be mostly independent, and remember, GTMO was a safe place where I didn't worry about them. I was able to hit the pause button to attend their activities when able, but I didn't have to drop everything to be omnipresent in their lives.

This sounds a bit terrible, but everyone could be happy—especially me. Even when I brought home work for evenings, weekends, and holidays, it didn't feel like work. That was the mindset I had grown to live with: I couldn't be happy unless everyone else was. Now, I truly enjoyed what I was doing—utilizing my educational pursuits and skills, attending change of command ceremonies, meeting new people and making a difference—and it became a sweet time for all of us.

Then, a shift occurred. As my career took off, Chris and I felt the ever-widening gap between us. It wasn't like in the past when I bowed to his wishes, fearful of being left to raise two girls alone. It wasn't like when I took the blame for any disagreement or even for his bullying. A new realization hit me like a wave of freedom. With this new career, the relationships I was building, and a newfound self-confidence, I found confidence to face Chris and his controlling behaviors while finally standing on my two feet, no longer cowering to the abusive tirades. I discovered I didn't have to listen to his cutting comments anymore. I no longer apologized for my success or pleaded for his understanding or support. I wasn't interested in the back-and-forth bickering. In the span of several weeks, it was as if I had grown up—finally. The fights didn't escalate; I was just more involved with my own life and self-discovery to care that he didn't like all the growth happening inside me. It was a redefining season for me as a woman, a mother, and a wife.

CHAPTER 8

IMMERSED IN WORK

"One of the greatest regrets in life is being what others would want you to be, rather than being yourself."
—**Shannon L. Alder**

June 2012

With time, I had landed a seat at the table, so to speak. In order to participate in certain meetings, I needed security clearance, something Chris envied. I had made friends at all levels of the military, and I often attended change of command ceremonies.

In the summer of 2012, GTMO experienced not only a change in command but a change in culture when Captain John Nettleton became CO of the base. Things started to feel different. It wasn't that the party atmosphere disappeared, but an era of accountability began.

A safe ride system was put into place, and DUI checkpoints were instituted across the base. If people were out at the bars, they could finally call for a ride to take them home, so the idea of drinking and driving became increasingly less acceptable. Eventually, the standard amount of acceptable drinking in any given sitting was lowered. The expectations dove so far that I was no longer comfortable having even one glass of wine at dinner and then driving home.

Chris and I were not sad about these changes to the GTMO lifestyle. We were parents first and foremost. Savannah was starting to drive, and Madison would often be trying to get home after a late movie, so I considered this change a blessing. I believed everyone's kids were safer than ever before now that people were being held accountable for drinking and driving.

Once Captain Nettleton and his wife, Leslee, arrived at GTMO, Leslee visited our offices at the Fleet and Family Support Center. When she walked through the doors, no one knew who she was because she looked just like one of us. Shorts. Casual top. As if she'd just stepped off an airplane (because she had). Human.

I say "human," because Leslee was personable, quite the opposite of many of her predecessors or the senior officers' wives, with their pomp and superior perspectives. Her down-to-earth attitude meant more to us than she likely ever realized. "You do know that when you leave this office, you won't be able to go anywhere, not even the grocery store, without people stopping you to talk, right? This will be the last time you walk in somewhere and no one knows your name." She smiled. She was so lovely, and I adored her from that day forward. There are few people in the world who, when we say, "they are so kind," we mean genuinely kind, all of the time. I never heard a snarky remark, nor anything rude, pass through her lips.

I attended Captain Nettleton's change of command ceremony. The only word I can use to describe it is *wow*. Set in the chapel, the entire event was beautiful and formal and lavish and splendid. (I guess I had a few more words in me.)

A few months later, there was another change of command ceremony to plan. This time, the Marine Corps would be welcoming a new CO. During this time at GTMO, Chris had spent a lot of energy becoming friendly with the Marines. Since he had been a former Marine, he wanted them to know they always had a friend in him. Right from the get-go, he helped with their holiday breakfasts, creating friendships and connections with anyone and everyone he could, including the sergeants and CO.

In late September, word circulated about the new CO coming down. Rumor was that he and his wife were newlyweds. And since GTMO always went beyond small-town America gossip, this new CO and his new bride were the talk of the base. I never liked the gossip, so when a coworker started in one day about how she believed his wife was a power-thirsty goddess who only married him because of his rank, I stood up and walked out. It was such a disgusting turn in office conversation. "How do you know that," I thought, wary of anyone who judges or makes assumptions about others. As the old adage goes, "When you point a finger at somebody, there are three more fingers pointing back at you." My heart hurt for this woman, whom I had yet to even meet. People were already gossiping, and she hadn't even arrived.

I ended up having lunch with the new CO's wife when they first settled on base, a recommendation and connection made by one of my coworkers, Angel. I was game. I had met my dear friend, Amy, the same way—through a mutual connection, a blind lunch—and we had been inseparable ever since. "Let's do this," I said to myself as I neared the restaurant.

Dawnell Pavao sat down at the table as she introduced herself, her Boston accent taking me by surprise. After an hour of conversation and finishing our meal, it was apparent she was not happy to be in Cuba.

She was thrilled to be married, but she had not been keen on the idea of being stationed at GTMO. She had a genuine way about her, and I knew right away I liked her. She wasn't fake and said what she meant. She didn't hide behind anything. I couldn't help but tell her what had transpired before her arrival. "You know what? You have a game to play whether you like it or not." I wanted her to know that her position, as wife of a CO, and the gossip that goes along with it was present before her plane had ever touched down.

Dawnell and I clicked, and from that point forward, we became inseparable—much like Amy and I had been—during our time at GTMO. It felt as if I finally had a choice in who to befriend. Dawnell became my trusted confidant, someone with whom I felt safe, respected, and empowered.

Chris and Dawnell's husband, Major Mark Cameron, connected and became best friends as well. The crowd we normally spent our time with shifted, moving from backyard social gatherings to dinners at the officers' club. Our routine remained consistent: work, go to a party, get drunk, and go home. But the group had changed. As CO of the Marine Corps, Mark and Dawnell led us to a different tier of socializing, and Chris relished that shift. After watching me mingle within the upper levels of the base, Chris had finally "arrived."

I continued to work at the Fleet and Family Support Center, and my classes grew. At times, upwards of 300–400 people, sometimes whole units, attended. I thrived in the excitement of building something successful. My superiors gave me more responsibility, and when 2013 rolled around, I noticed a slight bend in my career trajectory. The upper-level officers were including me in more conversations and decisions, and I received numerous accolades, outstanding reviews, and awards. It was more than self-satisfaction. I felt flat-out proud of myself. I had always known deep down I was more than capable of great things, but years of emotional let-downs and confinement to the role of wife—an abused wife at that—had left me without confidence. Until now.

The girls were on the honor roll at school. We had close friends in lofty positions. My career path was promising. Life was good in every way but with Chris and me. It felt as if he was fighting my success with every ounce of his being.

In the fall of 2013, the director of the center informed me she was taking another job. She wanted to groom me for her role, mentor me for the position of director. I started to shadow her, taking on more and working later hours. I brought work home at times, but that caused friction with Chris, so I stayed at the office as much as possible. I was exhausted, in essence working two forty-hour-per-week jobs. By December, I was acting director of the Fleet and Family Support Center at GTMO, and my eyes were set on securing the official position of director.

I slept less and rushed around much of the time, but I could not have asked for a better professional support system to guide me toward my promotion. Despite what many think or assume based on processes and procedures at other Naval bases, GTMO functions differently. I was somewhat of a lone wolf with some of the new responsibilities without the ability to look at how other bases did things, but the former director, now in Mayport, Florida, near Jacksonville, was only a phone call or email away. She supported me thoroughly, as did the XO, the executive officer, and other leaders at GTMO.

Chris's and my friendship circles had completely changed. Now, all of our closest friends were department heads—the public affairs office head, the CO of the Marine Corp and wife, and the department head from Personnel Detachment. We no longer hung out with anyone who wasn't considered a department head, not because we felt superior, but because we were always interacting with those upper levels, through both my work and our social network. We had found ourselves in a completely different realm at GTMO.

Chris and I tumbled downhill in our marriage during this time. I was now the head of a department, too, and he had been pushing so hard to be a significant force on the island, a "big man on campus." He worked as a loss prevention safety supervisor for the Navy Exchange. And he hated it. He had always wanted to be in charge, but I was the one who had ended up with a position of power. It had nothing to do with money—he still made more than me. It felt like we had made a one-hundred-and-eighty-degree turn within our marriage compared to the short couple of years before. In response, Chris tried to push his way into meetings and events where he didn't belong. I guess he felt entitled in some way.

My high-level position wasn't a problem for me. I felt my education and hard work warranted the transitions that were happening in my career. The problem rested solely with Chris. There were times he'd lie to people, telling them he had gone to college, even when that wasn't true. He also told people he had paid for my college when in reality, he never paid a dime. Down the road, I would learn he actually used my student loan money to pay bills. The cracks in his emotional stability widened.

It wasn't that Chris wanted me to be a full-time, stay-at-home mom. Our finances—and his lifestyle—wouldn't have permitted that set-up. His repulsion to my career was all about position and power. His "Nightingale" ego balked at not being able to say he provided for the family or that he was the point of power.

Over the next couple of months, this power struggle, Chris's bruised ego, and my new resolve to live my life for my own happiness caused the most harrowing roller coaster ride we had ever dealt with in our marriage. The conflict would cause me to become numb to Chris's emotional rants. I simply went through the motions: wake up, go to work, go home, go to bed, rinse, and repeat. I was always there for my girls, but with regards to Chris, I just smiled in public as Chris's "crazy" wife.

Spring 2014

Our family fractured into four pieces.

Savannah and I had gone on a road trip the year before to visit colleges. She was now a senior, and she was leaving home in the fall. Graduation activities were in full swing, and Madison was transitioning from middle school to high school. Our kids were growing up. There was so much change, and I believe Chris felt he'd lost control of everything.

I was waiting for the official word on my promotion to director of Fleet and Family Services. Chris marched into Captain Nettleton's office and demanded to know what was happening with my new role. Chris also shared with the CO that the promotion was destroying our home life. Later, I heard his exact words to the CO were, "(Explicative) or get off the pot."

Captain Nettleton asked him to leave the office with a polite warning, telling Chris the status of my position was none of his business. That didn't go over well with Chris. Paranoia set in like never before.

Embarrassed. Angry. Hurt. I felt all these things, knowing Chris had gone above my head and behind my back—and to the CO of the base of all people.

Chris had been told to get security clearance for his job since he was frequently over on the JTF side of the base. I didn't think much of it since I had security clearance for my job. Restrictions were getting tighter, but Chris dragged his feet. Instead of focusing on his own career, he hyper-focused on mine. It was my duty to report to high-ranking officers, but Chris saw it as clandestine work that I did behind his back.

As my confidential phone calls increased, he fumed. It became difficult to ignore his rage and his paranoid-infused suspicions.

Both of our drinking escalated. Mine to quiet his voice when he yelled. His in an attempt to regain control of his family and his life. I didn't want to be around Chris. On some level, he repulsed me. I didn't hate him; I hated being in his presence. His erratic behavior became too much to handle.

On one occasion, we were attending a concert on the base with our daughter, Madison, some friends, and hundreds of other servicemen and women. Chris stepped away from our group and beelined it to the bar. When he returned, a few service members, young enough to be my children, were standing too close to me—per his assessment—and Chris jumped to the conclusion they were getting "too friendly." He picked a fight—something he was doing more and more. "Why are you trying to (explicative) my wife!" he screamed. He jumped on one of the guys and punched him. Horrified, I tried to intervene, but our friends hastily pulled him off. There were kids all around us, watching.

"Come on! Really?" I thought, exacerbated. My cheeks flushed, not from the alcohol but from the shame I carried for Chris and our entire family. I've never wanted to run from a scene so fast in my life.

My role as director of the Fleet and Family Support Center was to exude friendliness and be welcoming to everyone on the base, no matter who they were. Chris was not only embarrassing himself and me, he was hindering my job.

Madison had been up near the stage, and thankfully, she was able to go home with the principal of the school and his wife. It allowed us to walk home, giving Chris the opportunity to let off steam and gain emotional control before stepping foot in our house. If he wanted to fight, I was the easiest target. He yelled at me almost the entire way. Eventually, I talked him down, as I had learned to do throughout our marriage, now nearly twenty years in the making.

He had become such a loose cannon that it started to happen more often in public. We were walking home from events and gatherings like this often. It didn't matter if I was in heels or if the road was long, Chris needed time to cool off. His justification sounded like this: "If you would just listen to me (or do what I say), I wouldn't have to do the things I do." I cringe hearing his voice and words in my head, even today. It used to be he'd have his meltdowns in the privacy of our home where he'd throw things and call me names. That was no longer the case.

If we were out at a bar, and he saw something he didn't like—a guy put his hand on my arm to order a drink over my shoulder or me talking with anyone else but him and our close friends—he couldn't keep it together. One evening, we were out with friends at a local bar. An "underground bar" had recently opened on the JTF side of the base called The Bear Trap. I was curious and wanted to check it out, so my girlfriend, Dawnell, and I told our friends and Chris we were going to head over there. I didn't feel I had to ask for permission. I was a grown-up. But Chris didn't see it that way. He had been suctioned to my hip for months now. In essence, Chris thought I needed a babysitter. I couldn't do anything or go anywhere without him.

"No, you're not going." Chris replied. His gaze bore into me, daring me to ignore him.

"I don't need your permission, Chris."

As I started to walk off, he threw his drink on me. Everyone at the bar stopped and eyed us. Mortified, I froze, wishing I had the ability to become invisible. I teetered between crying and stoic calm. He stormed out. My girlfriend sat with me and helped me clean off my shirt, trying not to draw any more attention from the crowd. But in the corner, I leaned into Dawnell and broke down.

"I'm not going to The Bear Trap, Dawnell," I said. Exhausted and burnt out from trying to keep peace while putting up boundaries in my marriage and my life, hopelessness pried its way back in.

As a superficial solution, I immersed myself in my work even more, and life wore on.

CHAPTER 9
THE ADMIRAL'S CALL

"Listen with curiosity. Speak with honesty. Act with integrity. The greatest problem with communication is we don't listen to understand. We listen to reply."
—**Roy T. Bennett** in *The Light in the Heart*

My work propelled me back into a zone. I developed two personas: "Before Five Lara" and "After Five Lara." On the job, I was professional, meticulous, and driven. After work, I had learned how to "let loose," and I built friendships and had fun with those who were authority figures between nine and five. I was able to compartmentalize my life into two periods of the day, and it suited me well.

In late Spring 2014, on a Friday night, Chris and I attended an Admiral's Call at the Officers' Club on the JTF side of the base, a place where we were members. Admiral's Calls were military versions of the civilians' Happy Hour, where everybody was invited to visit. The military takes a "public" stance against drinking, so you won't find much information about these events on the Internet. We received notification about Admiral's Calls through word of mouth since I was a department head, and Chris and I were friendly with JTF officers. Sometimes, these events were posted on the internal calendar. The Naval side hosted similar "Wardroom" events, and we were personally invited. The military paid dues for this group.

This particular night carried wall-to-wall people. The club was jam-packed, so we approached the bar before securing a table with our friends outside on the patio, which overlooked the water. On a clear day, we could see other parts of Cuba from this location. At night, we enjoyed the pleasant Caribbean breeze off the water, a lack of light pollution from any nearby city. The stars sparkled in the black sky.

Inside the Club, guests were greeted by a generous wrap-around, lacquered wood bar, complete with Jamaican bartenders we had all grown to love. You know you're a prolific drinker when the bartenders have your drink and an open tab waiting for you before you reach the stool of your choice. This was the case with us and our friends.

A small dance floor beckoned attendees from the middle of the room, alongside an area for karaoke. A couple of pool tables and tables for eating sat off to the side, and the room was made complete with lounge chairs and sofas. The space was not enormous, but it could accommodate most groups.

Most nights when Chris and I frequented the Club with our friends, it seemed empty, so we usually enjoyed the feeling of having a private bar. Other nights, the Club was crowded, loud, and exciting, like this night. Either way, I went there to avoid conversation.

Earlier on this particular Friday evening, Chris was less than enthusiastic about going to the Admiral's Call. When we arrived at the patio table after grabbing our drinks, he pushed me into the corner chair. It reminded me of "putting baby in the corner" from the movie, *Dirty Dancing,* and it made me feel as if I was his punished child. If someone wasn't a part of our group, he wasn't going to let me socialize with them. If you didn't come by our table, I wasn't going to be able to talk to you.

As the night progressed, we finally started to move around and walked outside for some fresh air. People were leaving the Club, and Chris and Mark announced they were going to The Bear Trap to continue drinking and hanging out. Dawnell and I were not invited. Dawnell wasn't even around us to hear their plan.

"What? No, 'Hey, do you want to come along?'" I felt the tug of resentment.

Chris knew I had not yet gone to The Bear Trap after the last time I mentioned checking it out—the time I ended up with his drink on my clothes. That didn't matter. The guys had their plan, and after a beat, I realized their escape would give me a chance to enjoy the rest of the night without Chris crawling up my backside, controlling my every move.

"You know what, go right ahead. Have a blast." My words had a bite to them. I was relieved, yet angry. They high-tailed it out without a second thought, leaving me to explain to Dawnell that Mark had abandoned her. She didn't take it well, angry that he had avoided her to hang out with Chris and a notoriously inappropriate woman, whom Dawnell had already confronted on a previous night about getting too chummy with Mark.

"Can you just let it go this one time?" I begged. "For once, Chris is not here."

She agreed. "I'll talk to Mark later."

An hour went by and the bar started to clear out even more. The only ones remaining were Dawnell and me, the Base PAO—Public

Affairs Officer—Kelly, her boyfriend, and a few stragglers. Ecstatic to have the Club to ourselves, we danced, sang karaoke, and drank for another half hour. The lovely bartenders from Jamaica cheered us on and smiled at our enjoyment.

In the mid-evening hours, the CO, Captain John Nettleton, rolled in. Up to this point, we had only built a professional relationship. We'd seen each other at social functions, but we had never really interacted outside of the office. Our kids went to school together. He knew "Before Five Lara." Returning from his own trip to The Bear Trap, the CO was not ready to conclude his evening, so he sat down and drank with us.

Several minutes passed, and the CO invited us all back to the dance floor.

"Let's go." I said. I was up for some more fun. I didn't think anything of it because the half dozen of us who remained hit the dance floor as a group. I knew the alcohol was influencing our interactions, but I didn't care. I was finally enjoying a night out, made possible because Chris wasn't glued to my hip.

Before long, it was only Captain Nettleton and I dancing—together. Somewhere in those moments, something happened. It's difficult to describe, and again, the drinking played a role, as well as my frustration about my relationship with Chris. It had been a long evening, but I suddenly experienced specific thoughts and feelings I had not had in years. The CO looked at me, not in a seedy or creepy way, but in a way that let me know I mattered to him. He stopped dancing. So I stopped dancing.

"You look incredibly attractive tonight."

My broken soul, the girl who had wanted to find worth, the woman who had endured so much emotional and verbal abuse, and the wife who had forgotten what it felt like to be seen as beautiful received a validating spark of adrenaline with that statement.

I believed him.

We were drunk, yes, but for the first time since Chris didn't recognize me in that airport terminal, pregnant with our first child, I felt attractive. It was flirtatious and fun.

We moved off the dance floor and sat again at the bar. No one else was seated around us, and in the next moment, he leaned over and kissed me. Shocked, I looked around to see if anyone had seen the intimate connection. No one had.

"You know I've been married almost twenty years."

"I've been married almost thirty."

I knew the past few minutes were wrong, but I was more confused than anything else. It was wrong, but it also felt right. Maybe right isn't the word. Good. The CO's attention and compliments felt good. I battled happiness and unhappiness; my feelings jumping between shock, elation, and fear. Then, it was as if a switch was flipped.

I looked at Kelly, kissing her boyfriend at the other end of the bar, and then looked around the room. I couldn't find Dawnell.

"Hey, Kelly! Where is Dawnell? I can't find her!"

Perhaps it was self-preservation. Perhaps it was guilt. Perhaps it was the need to do something different and redirect my thoughts, but I shifted gears. I went in pursuit of my missing friend. Whatever had occurred in those few moments had to stop, but it—all of it—would never escape me. I'd never forget how I felt, how feeling attractive was possible.

As I moved away from the barstool, I couldn't help but say these words to him: "You know. I think we're beyond me calling you Captain. I think I've graduated to calling you J.R."

That night was the last time I called the CO "Captain Nettleton" after five o'clock. I still maintained the professionalism required at work and called him "Captain." However, after hours, we became friends, and I referred to him as J.R.

As I looked for Dawnell, panic took hold of my gut. The night had taken a ridiculous turn. It had become a train wreck. Mark and Chris were still at The Bear Trap; J.R. was in poor shape at the bar; Kelly and her boyfriend were so intoxicated, I feared they might pass out at any minute, and while I was hours past drunk as well, I hit a moment of clarity. I knew something in my life had just been altered. I knew it even though I didn't know what was up or what was down.

I looked everywhere in the Club for Dawnell but couldn't locate her. Worried, I called Chris and Mark and asked them to come back.

"Can you guys take J.R. home? He needs help." I knew it wouldn't be appropriate or a good idea for me to take that task on myself. I wanted to find Dawnell. So I kept him at the bar until they returned, and when they did, they, too, were completely drunk. The three of them set off down the road, stumbling toward J.R.'s house.

By this point, my panic had escalated, and I realized I'm sober enough to know I'm not. Dawnell was still missing, and she was not answering her phone. I called Savannah, our teenage driver, to come and serve as a ride share for Kelly and her boyfriend. Realizing Dawnell was no longer at the Officers' Club, I jumped in the car with Savannah to help her.

We struggled to get Kelly and her boyfriend to Kelly's front door, and I worried they'd stay sprawled on the porch, passed out. But we both ran back to Savannah's car, and as she drove toward Dawnell's home, I hung out the window, calling her name. I didn't want to be so loud that we attracted the attention of the military police, but I shouted loud enough for Dawnell to hear me if she was on a side road or the sidewalk across the street.

We passed Chris, Mark, and J.R. meandering down the street. In his drunken stupor, J.R. yelled out, "She is so beautiful! Hey guys

[Chris and Mark], isn't Lara beautiful?" My gut clenched. From years of experiencing Chris's jealousy and paranoia, I wondered if he was sober enough to let the comment slide or so drunk a fight was imminent.

We found Dawnell. She had made it home and was nestled in bed. Irate doesn't begin to describe how I felt. Anger is so much easier to accept than fear, followed by intense relief. Anger covers the roller coaster of emotions with an easier ride to manage. I was grateful she was okay, but I resented the fact she hadn't let anyone know she was going to walk home by herself.

Then Chris called. Savannah and I now had to drive to J.R.'s house to pick up Chris and Mark. I assumed once they had deposited J.R. at his house, they would have walked home or at least gone back to the Officers' Club. Instead, the three of them had spent more time drinking together at Captain Nettleton's house. I will never know what words their discussions held, never discover what was said.

The next morning, J.R. called our house and Chris answered the phone. All I could hear was Chris's side of the conversation.

"Yup . . . Okay. Uh huh . . . No problem. Yep. Nope. Okay." Chris hung up.

"What was that about?" At once I wanted to know, but on some level, I also didn't.

"Oh, the Skipper wanted to know if he said or did anything inappropriate last night. I told him, 'Nope, you're good.'" That was all Chris said. He wouldn't tell me anything of what the three of them had talked about on their clumsy walk to J.R.'s home or while sitting and ingesting more alcohol.

I believed him because I had no other choice. To think J.R. would divulge the kiss would have rendered me terrified to be under the same roof as Chris. Chris never spoke about that evening again.

Beginning that morning, our marriage was effectively over. Chris's paranoia had taken such a turn for the worse—he moved inside himself, raging in places so dark and secret that he simply shut down. I had shut down, too. Our relationship broke into a hundred pieces.

Chris and Captain Nettleton's relationship was never the same, either. J.R. frequently witnessed Chris's harsh tone and scathing words to me in social circles. He saw Chris's public meltdowns. At one point, J.R.'s son ended up on the receiving end of one of Chris's drunken, vicious commentaries. His son was too polite to respond in any way, but J.R. never forgot it. J.R. remained professional, but the event certainly did not endure him to Chris.

And J.R.'s and my relationship had also changed. It was no longer simply a professional association. We became friends. Companions— drinking buddies—who hung out at social events, such as military balls and Wardroom events. It wasn't that I felt any kind of specific way about him. There was no sexual affair, but we talked a lot. We talked about our families and other relationships. About GTMO and our pasts. A close friendship had been born.

I didn't see J.R. and I as the problem to Chris's and my marriage. Chris and I were the problem. We had always been the problem. A marriage filled with distrust, disrespect, financial struggles, power struggles, and two decades of abuse had hit the point of no return, and we both knew it. Over the next six months, our marriage didn't deteriorate. It had already been over.

CHAPTER 10
STATESIDE

"Living with integrity means: Not settling for less than what you know you deserve in your relationships."
—Barbara DeAngelis

My relationship with J.R. grew deeper over the following weeks. Our flirtatious friendship aided me through long days, days spent walking on proverbial eggshells around Chris at home or avoiding him during work hours and beyond.

Chris and I kept up the appearance of a normal marriage for the girls and for social reasons. Savannah's graduation day arrived. GTMO's largest graduating class to date was set to enter the real world—a total of fifteen teenagers. The ceremony was absolutely breathtaking, held in the chapel, where the seats were packed with hundreds of proud family members and friends.

My parents and Ann, Chris's mother, had flown in to celebrate, and we threw a huge party for Savannah. Chris's birthday was on June 7, and that went by without much fanfare, causing him to throw a temper tantrum. I hoped he wouldn't take it too far with his mom around, but I also hoped she would just intervene and handle her son. His cyclical outbursts had moved from intermittent meltdowns to constant childish rants. I didn't bake him a cake, and he lost it. I tried to ignore him. I had other things to do—plan for our daughter's graduation party, host family and friends, and work. I didn't have the time, nor the desire, to celebrate his birthday by baking him a cake. His neediness repulsed me.

That summer was all about my girls. We had to pack up Savannah to move her stateside for college and Madison was entering high school. The kids were independent, but this was a big transition year, and I wanted to be present for it all and with them as often as possible. At this point, my two full-time jobs had finally merged into one—the official role of director of the Fleet and Family Support Center. I had a bit more breathing room with my time.

J.R. and I continued to interact at work and in social settings. The fact that the CO valued my professional opinion validated all the hard work I had done over the years. I valued his thoughts, too. His opinion of me mattered more and more because it was one laced with affirmation and respect. While J.R. is a very attractive man, it wasn't a physical connection that wooed me. It was the way he made me feel about myself.

Then, J.R.'s and my relationship escalated to include kissing. We were messing around, looking for more connection, but we didn't cross the line that defines sexual intimacy. The news media and others love to tell a story of an explicit affair, one where our sexual misconduct and teenage-like passion were out of control. The media knew their stories would thrive and sell more papers if they reported a "down and dirty, hot and heavy" scandal. But it just wasn't true. Yes, we were inappropriate. Yes, we were fooling around. No, we weren't talking about riding off into the sunset together or engaging in a sexual relationship.

There were multiple reasons why our friendship and physical connection blossomed. For one, J.R. and I were both in low places in our marriages and personal relationships. The difference was that J.R.'s wife, Leslee, was a genuinely good person. I liked her. A lot. On my end, Chris had been a nightmare from week one of our marriage when he belittled my apartment selection and called me lazy and fat. Chris continued to act like a child, and we were in our forties now. It was a stressful life, trying to avoid his cutting remarks and the objects he threw when he was angry. My relationship with J.R. was a safe place in which I could escape after so many years of being made to feel insignificant. J.R. provided security for me. It wasn't his position—though I was not in the military, my father served, and I have great respect for it. It was his compassion. And it wasn't necessarily his looks, though I would have noticed him in any crowd in other circumstances, especially in uniform. It was that I could freely express myself without criticism or admonishment. He made me feel better about myself.

Another point of misinformation that's been put out into the public was the reporting structure at GTMO. J.R. was a military officer. I was a civilian GS employee, a civil servant. I reported to somebody in Jacksonville, Florida. We worked in two different worlds. There's this idea, which surfaced after this story broke in the news, that because J.R. was the CO of the base, our relationship crossed professional bounds between superiors and subordinates. That somehow he abused his power against me. He had no hiring or firing control over my role or me. J.R. had no bearing on my job. This was not like the other high-profile cases of inappropriate relationships in the workplace that have made headline news.

I did not get my director job because of him. I applied through the proper channels, and I was more than qualified for the role. It was a role I had been groomed for over several years, and the awards and accolades I received were hard-earned and based on my merits. My promotion was a by-product of my abilities, and to think or say or write anything different is to tear away at a woman's—this woman's—hard work, and you'd be no better than Chris, or any other abusive man, who has held a woman back.

On the other side of this story, I did feel valued when J.R. brought high-level individuals, visiting from stateside, on tours across the base and included the Fleet and Family Support Center. The changes we had implemented over the years were a point of praise and pride. When J.R. congratulated me and complimented me on an intellectual and professional level, it fueled my attraction to him, especially when my husband continued to say my academic degrees and work at the center were meaningless, that I was a "worthless piece of (crap)."

People—all human beings—need to hear they are smart, cherished, valuable, important, and even beautiful. I realized during this time that one of my core needs is to feel that what I do matters, that it's significant. For decades, I had believed the lie, which stemmed from Chris's verbal and emotional abuse, that I was not worthy of praise. I was not important. No one cared about what I did. Appreciation. I missed that relational need. When J.R. offered that, I felt cared for. His acknowledging my professional successes and intelligence meant more to me than anything else I had ever received or experienced—from anybody.

I owed (still do) J.R. so much for helping me understand that I am worthy. With his friendship and affirmation, I began to put away the lies that had limited me over the years. Instead, I replaced them with his encouraging words. They were some of the most life-giving and powerful words I had ever heard. And I believed them.

I realized if I wanted to be a better person, a better mom for my girls, I couldn't stay where I was, accepting that I was fat or lazy, stupid or meaningless. I had not been showing my girls the best side of me. I regret that, even as I write this book. I regret taking so long to see Chris's dysfunctional lies for what they were, ways to control me and the girls. I hoped and prayed I could become the mom I was meant to be. I hoped and prayed my girls, now teenagers, could also reboot and rebuild, ignoring the way Chris had programmed their thoughts and beliefs over the years. I now knew there was more out there for the three of us, particularly me.

Because of all this, during that summer, the feelings of hopelessness and of being trapped began to dissipate.

J.R. had become privy to Chris's abuse. He listened without judgment. His kindness was a dressing to my wounded soul. At one point, he offered to help my situation:

"You know, I really need to report Chris for domestic violence."

I adamantly replied, "No. You can't." I explained that given the climate and culture at GTMO, Chris couldn't be reported. I knew from my own job that the military wasn't ready to handle this kind of situation safely or correctly. It was something I had been working on changing as director. My mission was both a professional and a personal one. "I know exactly what happens. It creates a huge domestic mess, and I don't want to deal with Chris and what he'd do if he were to be reported."

I knew it would become dangerous. I knew Chris would destroy my career. I knew he held my orders to live on the base, and without him, I would be kicked off the island. I would lose my housing and so much more. He was what the military refers to as "my sponsor." He had threatened me with that very truth on a regular basis over the years. It was one of the financial pieces he held over my head. "You should be grateful I even allow you to stay here!" he'd often yell at me in the middle of arguments.

I also wanted to maintain privacy. The GTMO rumor mill was vicious. I thought I could continue to "handle" things while Madison was still home and get her through high school. Savannah was leaving in a few short weeks anyway. I had to protect them, too. I understood the irony. I was the director of the Fleet and Family Support Center, a center with the vision to deliver "effective, life-enhancing services" to military members and their families. And I couldn't utilize the services for myself. I was trapped.

"If you report it, J.R., I'll deny it."

We worked out a compromise of sorts. I promised him that if I ever felt unsafe or if things were getting out of control, I would ask J.R. to figure out sponsorship for me to stay on the island, so I wasn't bound to Chris. I wanted to be able to stand on my own two feet, and as director and department head, I thought perhaps I would be able to hold my own sponsorship. I just needed a bit more time. J.R. relented. And I began to research ways to secure my future. Divorce weighed on my mind.

The time came to take Savannah to college. She had been accepted into the nursing program at a private university in Montgomery County, Pennsylvania, outside Philadelphia, on academic and athletic scholarships. She had played rugby at GTMO and was gearing up for lacrosse in college. The school was located close to Chris's mom, less than two hours from my brother and his family, and four hours from my parents, so I felt she'd have people to turn to in case of any emergency. Chris and I, after all, were living in a different country. We spent two weeks in Pennsylvania, staying with his mom, helping Savannah move in, and ensuring she had everything she needed.

My excitement for Savannah was palpable. Now a grown woman on her own, my heart carried both pride and sadness. I would miss her. But I knew she was ready to go.

Chris didn't share the same feelings about his oldest going off to school. Or perhaps he did, but the way he reacted to any negative emotions was to run away. He tried to do this very thing during these two weeks in the States. In the midst of moving Savannah into school, he said he wanted to go to Las Vegas.

"No, Chris. We're dropping Savannah off for college in a different country from where we live. We're not taking a vacation and leaving her here to move in by herself."

I didn't find it productive to get into the costs associated with the private university, the school and living supplies we had just bought for her first year, and the travel to and from Cuba. We had decent salaries, but I didn't see spending money to hightail it to Las Vegas as being good stewards of our hard-earned money. But Chris had never cared about the bottom line.

His mother overheard our conversation, which I was trying to keep from getting heated. I was unsuccessful, and Chris started in again with one of his full-blown tantrums—yelling, cursing, and pacing the room.

"Chris," his mom interrupted. "I don't think it's appropriate to go to Vegas right now."

"(Explicative) off!" he roared at her.

His mom screamed back at him, causing him to storm off to the bedroom in which we were staying.

"That's kinda how he's been," I offered in some attempt to explain, though I knew there was no justification.

"Wow," she replied.

Chris didn't emerge until the following day.

My family traveled down to wish Savannah well as she settled into college life. While in town, my sister-in-law pulled me aside.

"Are you distancing yourself from us because we couldn't go down to GTMO for Savannah's graduation?"

"Oh, gosh, no!" I said. "I'm not keeping up with anybody right now." I confided: "My life is a sh— show. There are things going on that you can't even imagine right now. It's not you guys. It's my life." I didn't have the energy to pretend anymore. My life battling Chris's outbursts and controlling rants sucked, and I didn't care who knew it. I was tired, frustrated that wives seem to always be the ones who have to explain and deal with all the "why" questions, apologize for the disappointments, and carry the burden of everyone's feelings. I wanted to scream, "Because my husband is a freaking nut job!" But I knew I couldn't do that, so I bit my tongue.

To appease Chris and his Vegas obsession, I suggested we visit Mark and Dawnell, who had been reassigned to West Point a month earlier, in mid-summer. Their change of command ceremony had been a month or two before we flew up to take Savannah to school. I knew Chris must be missing his best friend. I knew I was. I offered a plan that we take the subway to New York City, meet up with them, and enjoy a night out.

Chris seemed apathetic. Disappointed about not going to Vegas, I don't think any suggestion would have pacified him. But he finally acquiesced.

We ended up driving to West Point and reserving a hotel room just outside the campus. We met up with Mark and Dawnell and then toured the school and Mark and Dawnell's new place. Giddy with excitement, I anticipated a sweet reunion weekend with our closest friends. I had missed them dearly. My loneliness subsided as soon as I laid eyes on them. Dawnell had been "my person" for so long; we had been through a lot. I was tired of relying on Facebook and pricey overseas phone calls to stay close.

The first night, Chris relaxed a bit, and things were wonderful. This gave way to the idea of doing an all-nighter in New York City. Our plan was to experience the rolling nature of the city's nightlife, moving from bar to bar as one club closed and another opened, getting food along the way. We started at an Irish pub and moved on to a jazz club. Our goal was to find out if the old adage was true: Does New York City ever go to sleep? Looking back, I don't know why I expected the evening to go any differently than nights out with Chris and our friends on the base over the past couple of years.

At one point, we sat in a nice restaurant, eating dinner, when Chris piped up:

"I'm done. We're going home."

"What?" The three of us stared at Chris and then each other, each trying to determine what had sparked his sudden change and abrupt announcement. We had all been laughing just a moment before, and now Chris seemed angry.

"We're leaving," he said again.

There was no warning, no discussion. There had been no argument.

"No, we're not," I said. There was no explanation for this, so I wasn't about to cave. My heart ached to stay with our friends. "We came here to spend time with our friends and have fun." I was reminded of the abrupt way he had ended his welcome home party back when we were first married and he was home from Japan.

Chris stood and ran out of the restaurant. I excused myself with a quick apology and went after him. I knew Dawnell and Mark understood. They had seen this before.

When I reached Chris on the sidewalk, I asked what was going on.

"I said we're leaving, so we're leaving," he yelled. "I don't want to be here."

"No, we're not." I stood my ground. "We made plans."

Somehow, I convinced him to go back to the table and finish his meal. The four of us ended up visiting a few more places before Chris had another total meltdown. He screamed, paced the bar, and then he took off. We were in the middle of New York City, a place Chris and I were not familiar with, and he abandoned us. He took the only cell phone we had between us while we were in the States.

Mark tried to call him repeatedly, but he didn't answer his phone. Mark took off, hoping to find Chris, but he left Dawnell and me stranded with one phone that was low on battery life.

"That's just great," we said to each other. We found a small, well-lit eatery to sit and think. Time ticked by. My confusion turned to anger. It was just another example of a ruined evening at the hands of Chris's erratic behavior. I sighed and wrung my hands, and Dawnell looked at me with compassion, which just made me want to cry.

Mark called. He had found Chris arguing with a cab driver, but when Mark approached, Chris ran off again. This was all insane. I thought, "We're dealing with a child!" Part of me hoped he never returned. "Let him run off," I thought with fury.

Mark, Dawnell, and I decided to head to Grand Central Station, hoping Chris would be able to find his way there, too. When we arrived, we found Chris asleep on the grimy floor of the train station; people walked past him as if he were homeless.

"Hey!" I pushed on his shoulder to wake him up. "What are you doing?"

"Seriously? What's going on?" asked our friends.

Chris stood up. In the loudest voice he could muster, he screamed at me, calling me every name in the verbal abuse book. "You whore! You bit—!" The New Yorkers around us didn't even bat their eyes. This was nothing new to them. To this day, I don't understand why Chris was so angry. Embarrassed at the names he was throwing my way, I walked away from him. My heart pounded in my chest. Chris was way out of control—hands up, his face full of rage. He followed me. Fear set in. Would this be the time he finally hurt himself? Or me?

I escaped into the women's restroom, but it seemed to us all that he was going to chase me inside, still yelling at the top of his lungs. Dawnell inserted herself into the doorway, hand outstretched, to prevent him from pursuing me. I could hear them get into their own shouting match as I ducked further into the bathroom. Sweat poured down the back of my shirt. The musty air filled my lungs as I drew a breath to gain my composure. I wanted to turn invisible. To disappear forever.

Finally, Mark convinced Chris to walk away from the restroom. The train was coming, so Dawnell and I headed down to where the doors of the subway would open. The guys met us there.

While the train was pulling up, brakes echoing in the tunnel, Chris came up behind me and slammed me into the cement wall. He picked me up, as if hanging me on the wall, and planted his face inches from mine. He yelled again.

Mark grabbed him and threw him against the other wall. "Do you like that, Chris? I don't want to hear another word from you! Do not even think about touching Lara again!" Mark screamed at Chris before letting him go.

For the entire ride to our hotel, Chris was ordered to sit two seats behind us and keep his mouth shut. I sat with Dawnell, and Mark sat in front of us.

"Keep your hands still, don't touch Lara, and stay silent," Mark reminded Chris, talking to him as if he were a toddler in time-out. It seemed to be the only way to deal with Chris's behavior that night. We all sat in an exhausted stupor.

After a few minutes, Chris whispered to me:

"Are you happy? . . .

"Nobody likes me anyway . . ."

It was creepy. After a minute or two of this, Dawnell caught my eye and we smirked. It was all so ridiculous.

"Do you feel better because you got me in trouble with our friends?

"Eventually, no one else will be around . . ."

That last one sent chills down my spine.

"Shut up, Chris!" Mark yelled from his seat ahead of us.

When we arrived at our hotel, Chris made a beeline to our room without saying goodbye to Mark and Dawnell. He would never speak to them again. I apologized on his behalf, as I had always done. Hugging them good-bye, I turned around and went to our room.

Chris paced. We decided to check out of the hotel and make our way back to the Philadelphia area rather than sleep there. I welcomed that decision. I wasn't comfortable falling asleep with Chris in the room. His creepy whispers on the train played back in my head. I didn't trust him.

"Maybe on the way home I should drive us off a cliff and be done," he said. My eyes widened. Chris went on auto repeat, telling me how disappointed he was in me. "All I've ever done is love you. I've cared for you. I've put you on a pedestal. And this is how you pay me back? Why can't you just love me? . . . If you can't love me, nothing matters. There must be something wrong with you. I'm so disappointed in you."

Chris blamed me for the terrible evening. He blamed me for our terrible marriage. "Maybe I should just end it for the both of us," he threatened. I didn't want to listen to another word. But I had to or else risk sending him off the deep end again.

"Why can't you just respect me?" he asked. "The least you can do is show me some respect." His question became a statement, and he fell silent. I apologized over and over, trying to temper the situation.

I convinced him to let me drive home. There was no way I was going to get in a car with him behind the wheel. I deemed his threats credible.

As I drove, Chris repeated, "I'm disappointed in you," for nearly the entire trip from New York to the Philadelphia suburbs. It was a dark time, and I'm not referring to the wee hours of the night.

Finally, Chris dozed. I almost fell asleep behind the wheel. I had been awake for nearly forty hours. I decided to stop and catch a forty-five-minute nap while Chris slept hard. Then, I made sure we were back on the road before he woke up.

When we finally arrived back at his mom's house, I crashed into bed, not waking up until the following day. For the remainder of that trip, I put a smile on my face. It was the biggest dang smile I could muster, all in an effort to avoid any more confrontations or threats from Chris. If something made Chris happy, then for goodness sake, we were going to do it. I wasn't about to do anything to set off his anger before we landed in GTMO.

As we flew back home, I sat lost in thought on the plane. I knew I had to get my orders figured out. I had to find sponsorship. Chris couldn't be the one holding my life in his hands, not physically or financially. Not for one minute longer.

CHAPTER 11

INDISCRETION

"The one thing that doesn't abide by majority rule is a person's conscience."

—Harper Lee in *To Kill a Mockingbird*

Fall 2014

Upon our return from our eventful two-week period in the States, the tension between Chris and me transitioned to a more noticeable dynamic within the public eye. There were a couple reasons for this. Chris's out-of-control behavior escalated, though I didn't think that was possible at this point. The amount of drinking he engaged in was only matched by the number of meltdowns he displayed.

It was no longer a question of *when* he would lose control but *where*. His behavior was affecting all aspects of our lives, whether work-related or social circles. It seems we both had reached a point where we were no longer interested in hiding our struggles or saving face, not even Chris, who had tried so hard to be "the Joneses" on our street.

It wasn't that the past year and all its challenges hadn't elicited comments from our friends (they did!), but now it was becoming more obvious to outsiders that something was going on under the Tur roof. His inappropriate behavior sparked conversation about sensitive topics in many different networks. My emotional exhaustion hit a new level, but I still believed I could handle it all. Manage the outcome. In reality, my health deteriorated during this time. I experienced stomach issues and drank more while eating less. I suppose denial set in as another coping mechanism.

One evening, I went out with Kelly. Chris was there, too, but he was always there. At the end of the night, he became irate when I decided to go home with Kelly and not back to our house, where I didn't feel safe. Kelly agreed. Unfortunately, Chris followed us to her house, pushing in the door when she wouldn't let him in. He chased me through the hall, and I sought refuge under a table. As he typically did, he shouted venomous words, calling us both names. Kelly finally got him out of her house by threatening to call the police.

Chris went home where he lost it. Madison, who was home in bed, called me, begging me to come home. Chris was out of control, and she was scared. She had never been on the viewing end of one of his bigger meltdowns. She had always just thought of him as a drunk. On this night, he had gone home and started throwing things, destroying our property and waking her up.

"Mom! You gotta come home before he wrecks the house!" Madison cried. Panic and fear erupted in my belly. *My girl!* Kelly and I rushed to my home, just a few houses away.

Kelly pulled Chris onto the porch, and they spoke for a long time. I consoled Madi, realizing we were failing her. The pain in my heart was indescribable. I didn't know how to help her feel safe; I didn't know how to help myself feel safe.

I picked up the house, glancing outside every once in a while at Kelly and Chris. Later, she would tell me he kept saying, "She doesn't love me anymore. I love her so much, but it's not worth going on if she doesn't love me. She's my life. I don't know what I'm going to do."

Chris agreed to go see the chaplain on base for a session of counseling. Kelly thought he had calmed down enough for her to go home. Madison was half asleep in her room. We all assumed Chris would sleep it off, as usual.

As soon as Kelly closed our front door, Chris turned to me. He tore off the mask, like so many times before, and laid into me again. He picked up his bottle of Jack Daniels and slurred hateful words my direction. Then, in what seemed like an instant, he switched gears:

"I took a bunch of pills, Lara. I'm going to end it all right now. If you're not going to be with me, there's no use in living." I wasn't going to play his game and get into another argument. I knew this was about control. It wasn't the first time he had used threats of suicide to get me to say and do what he wanted.

"Chris, stop it. I'm not doing this. I'm not going to listen to it. Take the couch. Take our bed. I don't care. You're drunk. Just go to bed." He refused.

I went into Madison's room to sleep next to her, leaving Chris with his bottle of Jack. I lay next to my daughter, who had witnessed his violent outburst for the first time, and I prayed. I was done apologizing to Chris. I hadn't done anything wrong. No one deserved to live like this, especially our daughter.

A few minutes later, Chris texted me.

I'm in the garage. I'm going to kill myself.

I threw my legs over the side of Madi's bed and crept out of her room. In the garage, I found Chris. The car was running, and the garage door was open. In that instant, I knew it was another grandiose display. Another game. If you want to put on a show for someone, if you want to make them crazy, that is how you do it. No one is going to die sitting in a car in a garage with the garage door all the way up. He was beyond drunk.

Chris jumped out of the car and threw himself on the concrete.

"Why won't you just love me? I do everything for you! Why can't you just love me back!" Chris repeated as he curled into a ball.

"Chris, that's it. I'm calling the hospital. We need to get you some help. You've now said you're going to kill yourself and moved to do so." Working at the Fleet and Family Support Center, I had the hospital's number in my contacts. I pulled out my phone and tapped my contacts app.

Chris jerked himself upright and took off.

He didn't return that night.

Many years later, I would find out that Chris had staged a whole scene in front of Madison before Kelly and I had arrived, professing his good-byes to her and drinking from a Captain Morgan bottle. He had moved to unplug all the house phones. That was when she had panicked and called me.

Madi talked about her fears with Kelly and would, in the years to come, testify in a grand jury about this night. Because we would be told not to communicate with each other during legal proceedings, I did not find out about Chris's horrific theatrics in front of our daughter for quite some time. Even years later, I sobbed for Madison. For my child and for me, as a victimized mother who didn't know where to turn for help.

Throughout the evening after Chris ran from our driveway, I paced outside, in our front and back yards, thinking, "What in the world?" I had tried several times to call and text Chris without any luck.

Please come home. I'm sorry. This isn't necessary. We can work it out.

I left a dozen messages on his voicemail.

As I was listening to the ringing on the other end of one of my desperate calls, I stepped back inside our house. It was then I discovered Chris had left his phone at home when he had run away. My stomach dropped. I grabbed his phone and shoved it in my pocket.

The following day was the start of Customer Appreciation Weekend, and Chris was scheduled to work at a "color run" 5K event, one starting fairly early in the morning. When he didn't show up, the Navy Exchange office called me, asking where he was. I had no answers. This was unlike Chris. Even with his alcoholism, even with his erratic behavior, Chris had always gotten to work, ready to do his job. He was professional; it aligned with his desire to be "Mr. Jones," someone everyone wanted to emulate. The perfect employee. The perfect family. The perfect life. He had always lived by the military's mantra, "If you're on time, you're late." My heart beat double-time with this call.

When I hung up with the Navy Exchange, I called Kelly. I explained he had left the night before and told her about the ominous texts and the fact he never made it to work.

Kelly came right over, and we headed out to search for him, starting with the marina. Chris and I owned a boat at that point, and he would sometimes hang out there, fishing or thinking. Sometimes cooling off from one of our arguments. Some of the roads were blocked with the color run event Chris was supposed to be working.

Chris wasn't on the boat. I pulled out my phone and called Chris's friends and others who might have known his whereabouts. No one had seen him. Kelly and I decided to check the hospital. We figured we could ask about any "John Does" who may have been dropped off or come in overnight. Chris had been so drunk the night before, I thought maybe he had passed out and someone found him. We didn't want to use Chris's name and risk his career.

Just as we entered the hospital, Chris called me. There was no greeting.

"Do you have my phone?"

"Yes," I replied.

"I need my phone for work," he spit out.

"Okaaay," I said slowly. I pushed my anger down. I thought, "No 'hello?' No 'I'm sorry?' No, 'I'm okay?'" *Unbelievable.*

Chris gives me orders. "I'm going to be home in ten minutes. Just bring me my phone." When he arrived through the door a minute after Kelly and I had walked in, he went to the bedroom, changed clothes, grabbed his phone, and walked out. No words were exchanged between us. That was it.

When Chris came home after his work shift, I asked, "Where were you last night?"

He wouldn't give me specifics. He only revealed he had camped out fifty yards from the house and watched me all night long. I couldn't believe he had seen me pacing, worried, and he never came out. My jaw clenched. I hated that he had let me agonize about his whereabouts all night long. It was another control tactic.

"You need help," I said through my teeth. "It's no longer an option."

———

Chris started going to behavioral health at the base hospital and made an appointment with the base chaplain. We had tried marriage counseling in the past, and it had never ended well. On one occasion, Chris had become so defensive about what the counselor was saying, he had stood up, walked out, and didn't just sit in the car to wait for me, but drove away, leaving me stranded at the counselor's office.

I decided to go with Chris to the first session with the chaplain. I knew the chaplain from my role at the Fleet and Family Support Center, and I had even attended a few of his Sunday sermons over the years. I liked him and had enjoyed his sermons, even though I typically attended a church of a different denomination. Jesus doesn't care where we go to spend time with him.

During this session, I thought this might be the one and only time I had to say what I was truly thinking and feeling. I assumed it would be Chris's first and last session, given his history with counseling.

The chaplain asked us why we were in his office. I didn't hold back.

"This isn't about me at all," I said. "I know I have some of my own issues, which I'm happy to admit to, but they're mine to handle right now. After all these years, we're here for Chris. I have put up with more physical, financial, emotional, and verbal abuse than any spouse should ever experience. I'm not sure our marriage is worth salvaging." There. I had said it. I had finally admitted to someone besides a couple close friends who had witnessed some of the abuse over the years, that I was the victim of an abusive spouse, and we had a toxic relationship. And for the first time, Chris did not deny it. He openly spoke about being a bad husband and that he was abusive. I felt the weight of perhaps one of twenty years of silence slip off my shoulder. It landed in silence.

The chaplain wanted to know if I was open to marriage counseling.

"Honestly, we've tried that. So, no," I said bluntly. "I'll support his individual counseling," I added.

"If you see Chris make some changes, would you be willing to receive them?" asked the chaplain.

"I don't know." At this point, after so many years, it was as if a switch had been flipped. I felt numbness. Actually nothing. Twenty years was a long time to work toward reconciliation and forgiveness, especially when the harm continued. I was broken, and I just wanted to be whole again. I did not think that wholeness could involve Chris as my husband. I wished he could sober up and stop the abusive behavior, but deep down, I didn't think he could change. I didn't hate him. I hated what he had done to me.

I explained to them that sorry was such an overused word in our relationship. I didn't believe it anymore, and I had become immune to his manipulative words and actions.

The chaplain gave Chris some "homework." He told him to write love notes to me and leave them in random places for me to find. And whether I reacted negatively, responded positively, or did nothing at all, the chaplain instructed Chris to keep writing them.

Just as with anything Chris had done over the years, he started off writing genuinely reflective and meaningful letters. I could tell he was putting some thought into them. But it wasn't a week or two before the tone of the notes changed. The content of his letters moved from kind messages about what he was learning through all this to what he expected of me in return for receiving these letters. His notes turned creepy.

Not only did his notes reflect his underlying dysfunction, but I started to notice him throughout the day watching me, in places he had no business being. My husband was now stalking me. At work. Running errands. Out with friends. I saw his red Jeep nearly everywhere I went. When I worked late, I caught him casing my building when I went outside for smoke breaks. My office wasn't in a location where Chris ever needed to be, so there was no room for coincidences. I felt like a caged animal.

While he stalked me in private, his romantic overtures became public. His goal was to paint the picture of a doting husband while behind the scenes, every gesture had intent. Threat aimed at me: *You're not only mine; you're trapped.* And a message to others: "This is *my* wife." It felt possessive—as if he were a dog, marking his hydrant with urine.

Another example was the effort he took to deliver flowers to me on the island. In Cuba, getting fresh flowers is not only an expensive endeavor, but a chore of sorts. The base was too isolated. So Chris went to work planning: He conspired for people who were flying into GTMO soon to bring me a dozen red roses. As the flowers came off the plane, of course, everyone wanted to know who they were for and who had sent for them. Chris became a local hero. What nobody else realized was that I hate roses. Chris knew this. We had been married for twenty years. He knew in year one of our marriage that roses didn't do it for me. The card said, "I love you." The unwritten message was, "I'm in charge. I don't care about you." My insides turned upside down. It was all so alarming, and fear nestled itself deep in my gut. "I might be in real danger here," I thought.

Meanwhile, my friendship with J.R. continued. I was terrified of flying, and he and I would joke about him taking me up in his C-13, a small plane. "I don't even like big planes," I'd laugh. "Heck no."

It was during this time when Chris started stalking me—leaving flowers on my car to let me know he was there—that a training session opened up in Jacksonville. I was interested in attending. It was for new managers in government roles, and while I had been in supervisory positions in the past, as director, this was the first time I was in a governmental management role. I was granted permission and made the comment to J.R. that I was heading to Jacksonville for this course.

"How about that," he replied. "I am going to an engineering symposium in Jacksonville that same week."

"Wow. Isn't that amazing?" I chuckled. It had worked out for us to be off the island at the same time, and I was excited to be free from my cage for a short stint. I flew to Florida at the end of October on a Friday since flights in and out of GTMO only occurred on Fridays and

Tuesdays. I would have the weekend in Jacksonville to relax, shop, and prepare for the training sessions.

When I arrived, my government credit card wasn't working, so I had trouble checking into my hotel. Since it was Friday afternoon, no one was at the business office at GTMO. I sat in the hotel lobby to figure out what to do. Chris called as soon as I sat down.

"Why haven't you called me yet?" he said with a nip in his words. No "hello." No, "How was the flight?"

"Chris, I can't do this right now. I just got to my hotel, and my card isn't working. I can't even check in."

"What do you need?"

"I need to talk to the comptroller, but it's after hours. I can't get ahold of her."

"Well, you're in luck. I'm sitting at the bar having a drink with her right now."

"What?" *Really?* The double-standard whacked me in the face. Since we had met and married, Chris and I had a standing rule to protect our marriage—no going to bars to drink when the other is off the island. If the roles had been reversed, he would have gone nuts, likely flying back to GTMO at first chance to "teach me a lesson." Just a few months back, I had gone out—as the designated driver—with Mark and Dawnell without Chris, and he had been irate when he found out, even though this couple was a mutual friend of ours. I believed his behavior now was payback, juvenile revenge.

As soon as the anger hit me, it subsided. I found that a bit strange, but I realized: *I no longer care what he does.* I just didn't give a dime anymore.

"Just make sure you know where Madison is while I'm gone," I said, knowing I had to play the role of parent even while gone.

The card error was rectified, and when I entered my hotel room, I was met by the largest vase of flowers I have ever seen. The flowers stood three to four feet tall. At first, I thought they were part of the hotel decor because the vase was so big. Then, I saw the card poking out. *Chris.*

"This is ridiculous," I sighed. I unpacked and started to hang up my business clothes. That's when I saw the note from him in my luggage. That creepy tingle went up my spine. He had gone through all my things. I had no privacy left. None.

I wasn't in the hotel room more than five minutes when Chris called again.

I answer without words.

"Are you going to say thank you?" he snarls.

"Chris, I've been here five minutes. I'm coming off my medications for flying," I started in with the justification. Then, I realized I was the one being ridiculous. I had nothing to justify.

His anger was palpable through the phone. "That's what you say? I give you flowers. I give you notes, and all you can say is you're coming off your medication?"

"No, no. I'm sorry. They're beautiful. Thank you." I didn't have the time nor the energy for this. I appeased him so that I could move on with my weekend. I even put a picture on Facebook for him to see. Dawnell, who knew the drill, knew about his controlling behavior, and knew what to do instantly "liked" the photo so he would be pacified. The games we all had to play!

I called Madison, said goodnight, and went to bed.

On Monday of that week, I worked in my former director's office, caught up with her, met new people, and scoped out space for my future. I envisioned some day following in her footsteps and working in the Jacksonville area.

The training started on Tuesday.

Late in the day on Tuesday, I stood outside the hotel lobby, smoking and talking to Chris on the phone when J.R. and two other men walked up. They had just arrived for their symposium. I said hello to them as they approached.

"Who is that?" Chris demanded.

"It's J.R. and some others," I replied. Chris and J.R. exchanged a greeting through me, and the men invited me to a drink later in the evening at the bar.

I declined, but Chris said, "Go on. It's better than drinking alone." I thought it was strange that Chris communicated that perspective. I called it for what it was—a dicey game we were now both playing, but if he was going to offer it, I didn't argue.

That evening, I got dressed and headed to the bar. It was quiet. The three men were seated off to the side in the corner of the bar. I passed the two men I knew by name and recognition—one military, the other a civilian—to find a seat next to J.R. I don't know if the two men thought anything strange about that or not. It was obvious I knew J.R. and had just met them in person, so I didn't think anything of it. When I look back now, I suppose it could have seemed awkward for me to walk all the way around them to sit next to J.R. You just never know how things will roll off people.

After a few drinks and conversation all around, one of the men excused himself to go to bed. Then, J.R. said he was going back to his room to get some sleep, too. I sat and chatted with the third man, the civilian, for maybe twenty more minutes. Then, we called it a night, as well.

During the course of the evening at the bar, J.R. and I had exchanged hotel room numbers. I didn't think anyone else had heard us do so since the other two were having their own conversation at the time. A few minutes after I returned to my room, I heard a knock. I opened the door to find J.R. standing there, smiling.

I smiled back.

The bars of my cage disappeared when he walked into my hotel room. He shut the door, and we enjoyed what was for me, the most amazing night of connection with another human being I had ever experienced.

I know everyone wants to read about the details, a more salacious scene, here. It's what makes headlines. Trust me, I know. But that would detract from my emotional connection with J.R. and with the re-discovery I experienced for myself. This was a highly personal and defining point in my life. I had moved from feeling like a caged animal to freedom, even for just a few hours.

It wasn't like I was some flirtatious schoolgirl and he, my knight in shining armor. I knew this wasn't about someone sweeping me off my feet and us riding off into the sunset. I wasn't naïve. I held no misconceptions, never thought J.R. would drop everything, leave his wife, or lose his career for me. I didn't feel anything. I didn't think anything. I didn't think about anyone. I just let go.

Years of torment, abuse, fear, and feelings of unworthiness dissipated that night. While it was impulsive, it was also liberating. It didn't feel like a cliché. It was intimacy, respect, and freedom rolled up into two people's shared encounter.

What was infinitely more important than the physical connection was my realization that I was worth it, worth anything. I knew I was wasting a lot of my time, my life, with someone who didn't care about me. Worse, who abused me. That night confirmed my belief that I owed it to myself and to my girls to change my life. I wasn't a good role model for them, and I didn't want them to think that love was painful or domestic violence was normal or acceptable. I knew I had been drinking too heavily for many years. I knew my life was a mess; but now, I had hope for something better.

That night, I believe J.R. and I were just both in bad places relationally. Professionally, our lives were wonderful, but inside, I think we both were struggling. I would never and will never speak for him, but I don't think you end up where we did that night if you're in a great place in your personal life.

I don't view J.R. as a bad person for knocking on my door. That night, for me, was about me and only me. I moved from being a hollow shell of my former self to someone who might now be able to grasp her own identity and humanity. I enjoyed being wrapped up in that moment, thinking my life was different than my reality. I could have stayed in Jacksonville, in that hotel room, forever. Sad when I eventually had to leave, I don't think there are words worthy of how that night changed me. I'm still processing it all five years later, and I will always cherish those memories.

There are people who want to make it out that I was (and am) delusional, believing J.R. would "rescue me" from Chris and that somehow I thought this was the start of a new, long-term, and public relationship. Those people aren't me. They aren't J.R. They weren't privy to our inner battles or our external situations. We are the only ones who know the significance and details of that night.

On Friday, I flew home, feeling a mixture of deep sadness for the cage to which I was returning and hopeful energy for my newfound understanding of my own worthiness.

CHAPTER 12

RINGING IN THE NEW YEAR

"You can fool some of the people all of the time, and all of the people some of the time, but you cannot fool all of the people all of the time."

—Abraham Lincoln

When I returned to GTMO, everything seemed different—odd might be the best word. It was as if a thin layer of plastic had been added to the world, leaving colors a bit less bright. Fuzzy. Chris's paranoia and stalking resumed in full force. I loped back into my cage.

The day I returned from the airport, Chris was home alone and wanting to engage in sexual intimacy. Madison was gone, and he had turned on music from his iPod, docked in its station. I wasn't in the mood, but it didn't matter.

Suddenly, the song, "I Know I'm Not the Only One" by Sam Smith played from the iPod. I had never downloaded that song before, a scary reminder that Chris, if he should ever discover what had happened in Jacksonville, would lose it, likely leaving me injured or worse. I wondered why he had it queued up. Was it a warning? His sexual advances became animalistic. I felt awkward, used, and manipulated.

The Marine Corps Ball loomed right around the corner. I had gone shopping for ball gowns in Florida. We had attended many of these balls over the years; they were opportunities for us to get dressed up—social occasions unlike any others. This time, I didn't feel like engaging in the fanfare. I wasn't in the mood to be social, get dressed up, and pretend everything was okay. Nonetheless, we went, and I know I wasn't my usual upbeat self.

I wasn't eating but simply sitting at our table. Looking back, I guess I was sad and tired, emotions not fit for a Marine Corps Ball. My movements were mechanical, born from years of going through motions. I had also been drinking, trying to numb the negative feelings and avoid the realization that my marriage—and life—was a lie. The pre-ball photos showed me in a fancy dress, smiling and ready for a night out. The photos taken during the ball, which would be given to me two months later, certainly depicted the amount of alcohol I had consumed and the hopelessness of my outlook. A drunk Cinderella.

At one point during the evening, I walked into a conversation between J.R. and Chris. As we had all done for years, light-hearted and crass jokes flowed between the couples at the Officers' Club. When I stepped into their space that night, I heard Chris ask how I was on the C-12 flight home from Jacksonville. There was no secret about my fear of flying; I believed he simply inquired for that reason, but I panicked. Chris told J.R. my flight medication usually makes me pass out, saying,

"If she's not restrained, she'll fall right into your lap." He laughed. But it was J.R.'s response that escalated the conversation and my panic erupted into full-blown terror.

"I wouldn't mind her head in my lap."

My jaw dropped and Chris's face flushed fire. In a normal friendship at GTMO, this comment would have gone into the "haha lane," but this was no normal social circle.

No, not tonight.

"I need to leave." I stepped away quickly, praying Chris wouldn't erupt, but it was too late. We kept drinking, but eventually, he entered into typical meltdown mode, and we hastened home. Thankfully, Madison was spending the night with a friend. Chris wanted to fight all night long.

"Why don't you love me?" he screamed.

"We're calling J.R.'s house and talking to Leslee." Chris was furious about J.R.'s comment. I begged him not to do such a thing, to involve two whole families in something so inconsequential.

He acquiesced.

For the next few weeks, I struggled with getting to work. Chris wanted to talk and argue, starting discussions at ten or eleven o'clock at night that went into the early morning hours. I lost sleep, and experienced more migraines and tension headaches. I called in sick or showed up late often, which was not normal for me. I had always been on time, professional, and reliable. I didn't know what to do. I just kept coddling him, trying to pacify him so I could find some rest.

"Why don't you love me?" he continued to ask me. I had no answer for him.

Finally, in the first week of December, there was a tipping point. I had just called into work, saying I'd be late again as I wrestled with another headache. Madison had already left for school. I gripped the phone as I spoke to Kelly, telling her I had to call in late again because of Chris. He was in the background, slamming doors and yelling obscenities at me.

"Why do you always have to call a friend!" he shouted at the top of his lungs.

I hung up the phone, and we both ended up in our bedroom. I stood by the door, and Chris sat on our bed. We were deep into yet another argument about why I didn't love him and how he was preventing me from doing my job.

"Chris, it's over. I want a divorce," I said the words I had been thinking for years. "I don't want to do this anymore."

"No," his one-word response was simple yet laced with rage.

"We've grown apart. We can be adults here. I don't want to be married to you anymore."

"No."

"Chris, stop. I'm not asking for child support or alimony. I'm not asking for anything. It's not about anyone else. I just don't want to be married."

"No." He stared at me. My heart raced, and I readied myself for a backlash. "If you try to divorce me, I'll ruin you. I'll make your life miserable." His voice was calm, which made the words scarier.

"Chris—"

"If you try to divorce me, I won't pay for Savannah's college."

"What if Savannah meets someone, and he talks to her like you talk to me?" I asked.

He didn't skip a beat with his answer. "Well, if she behaves like you, she'll deserve it."

I couldn't believe what I had just heard. And yet, it all made sense. He knew it would hurt me. It had come to this, him using the girls against me.

"Okay. I can't do this with you. Nobody deserves this." My time reflecting on what I wanted in life, who I wanted to be, and the type of role model I wanted to be for my girls buoyed me.

"I told you what will happen if you try to divorce me." His threats continued. Somehow, I knew this conversation would stay with me for the rest of my life. I inched closer to the doorway, ready to bolt if I felt any more threatened. His voice was so cold and so confident, like he knew he'd never lose, that he owned me forever. There is nothing more frightening than knowing you can never leave.

"Fine, Chris. Let's do this: I'll give you thirty days. One month. Savannah is coming home next week for Christmas break. I want to enjoy the holiday with our daughters. For one month, no fighting. No talking or late-night arguing. No talk about divorce.

"Let's both think about this like adults, and let's take this time to consider next steps. We have our whole lives ahead of us. Let's take a month and then go from there. Let's enjoy Christmas as a family."

I knew a month would buy me time to figure out Savannah's college expenses. I could talk to people about a loan or consider using my 401K. I wanted to plan for the financial piece of leaving Chris, the one he had held over my head for far too long.

Chris agreed to the thirty-day plan, but with stipulations. I had to agree to act "like a wife." He laid out what he meant:

- *I had to kiss him when I left for work.*
- *I had to kiss him when I returned home or when he returned home if I was there first.*
- *I couldn't work past 5:00 p.m. or on the weekends.*
- *I was to notify him if I had to leave the office for a meeting and then tell him when I returned to my office.*

- *If he called or texted, I was to answer my phone or respond immediately. If I didn't, he would call my staff to find out where I was and what I was doing. If they didn't answer, he would come to my workplace and find me.*
- *I had to engage in "a wife's bedroom duties" with him whenever he wanted—no complaints, no excuses.*
- *He wanted to know my every move for the next thirty days.*

I agreed, bile moving up my esophagus. I had no choice. These were his non-negotiables, and I didn't think there was anything to counter with. My girls and I were bound to him for sponsorship and a host of other financial reasons, and I feared what he would do if I didn't agree. It was December 11, 2014.

I shared the thirty-day plan with a couple of my girlfriends. They thought his requirements were ridiculous, though I suspect they didn't understand the full measure of his control or what it felt like on my end.

During the second half of December, while the base didn't shut all the way down, we were on reduced hours. Many of my staff members took time off, and so did I. We rotated our weeks on and off to ensure the support center was covered. But scaling down was something every department did during the month of December. This was part of the reason I agreed to Chris's demands. I knew I wouldn't be at work as often as normal during the next thirty days.

December also meant many people left the island to visit family and friends stateside. There wasn't much to do on base, but this gave me time to spend with my girls. Savannah had made it home from the States, and even though both girls hung out with friends, I enjoyed the time we had together.

I played along with Chris's thirty-day rules throughout the holidays. Chris did, too. Meaning, he didn't start fights or ask me why I didn't love him. In some respects, I caught a glimpse of what Chris could be like if he wasn't tormented by his outbursts, emotional immaturity, and violent tendencies. However, as always happened, as soon as I was able to see any respectable qualities, Chris would do something to erase any hope I harbored.

He and Savannah, as they did when she was younger, butted heads often during Christmas break. She had reached an age of maturity and had been away from home for the first time, so I believe she had also come to the realization she didn't have to tolerate his "king of the castle" bravado. I was inwardly proud of her.

Christmas came and went, and we planned for the New Year's Eve celebration. Madison had taken a babysitting job for the night, so Savannah, Chris, and I attended the party and fireworks event out on the patio at the Officers' Club. I had decided not to drink that night. I just wanted to have a nice time and spent much of the evening with Savannah, who wasn't old enough to drink anyway. We enjoyed each other's company, catching up and chatting about anything and everything. A part of me didn't want her to leave on the eighth, but I could see she was thriving at college.

They say whatever you're doing at the stroke of midnight on New Year's Day is the preamble to the year to come. As the night wore on, I lost track of time. A few minutes before 12:00 a.m., I headed to the restroom. Just as I flushed the toilet, I heard the emcee on the microphone: "Three . . . two . . . one! Happy New Year!"

"Oh my goodness!" I ran out of the bathroom, desperate to find Savannah and Chris, though inwardly, I chuckled at the timing of it all. When I reached Chris and Savannah, I told them where I had been, and we all laughed at the thought of me in the bathroom as the New Year rang in.

If I had known how bad 2015 would become, I wouldn't have been laughing that night. I was on the proverbial "pot" for the first tick of the New Year, and less than two weeks later, events would take a horribly wrong turn. 2015 was about to go down as the worst year of my life.

CHAPTER 13
HAIL AND FAREWELL

"Develop enough courage so that you can stand up for yourself and then stand up for somebody else."
—Maya Angelou

When we returned home after the New Year's Eve party and fireworks had concluded, we decided to play a board game in an attempt to do more family-oriented activities before Savannah's departure. As a family, we frequently engaged in board and card games. It was one of "our things."

Chris's uber competitive juices were flowing, as usual. When you play with someone as cutthroat as Chris, you typically don't worry about the official rules. And we didn't either. We usually played by the "house rules." And when you play "house rules," there is often someone who decides to bring out the official rules pamphlet when questions arise. There are memes about this, so I know we're not the only family to whom this happens.

On this night, Savannah pulled out the official rules.

"That's not how you play," she said to Chris as she located the game booklet in the box. "Either play the right way or don't play at all," she continued.

Chris's face contorted into a snarl, his eyebrows pinching together in the center above his nose. He didn't like being questioned. "Shut your (explicative) mouth," he said to her.

I froze. My mind raced even though my body had gone still. "That is not okay," I thought, afraid of what might happen next.

Savannah stared her father down. At five-foot-six, she was taller and bigger than me, who stands five feet, four inches when standing up straight. "You cannot talk to me that way," she calmly replied. "It's not okay."

What? Where did she learn how to stand up for herself like that?

Their voices rose.

"You're being a bi—, Savannah," Chris retorted.

Standing, she replied, "I don't have to listen to you. If you're going to talk to me that way, I won't sit here." Savannah headed to her bedroom and closed the door.

As I watched her walk away, I realized I stared at a mature woman, one for whom I felt an immense amount of respect. She had been stern, confident. And she was so very right. She was no longer a kid; there was no stomping of feet or slamming of doors. She had grown up. "Good for you!" I silently cheered, hoping she understood how proud of her I was at that moment.

Chris looked as if he had been slapped in the face. His cheeks and neck turned crimson, and his hands balled into fists. He turned to me as if expecting me to defend his position or tell Savannah she was wrong. I would do no such thing.

Savannah, I did not teach you that. I wish I had. I would be in a better place today had I learned how to do that a long time ago. Good for you!

Game night was effectively over. And the next morning, no one said a word about the interaction. It was another typical Tur cover-up.

It was still the first week in January. Chris and I had gone out to a bar. I can't remember if there was a specific occasion or if we were with friends that night. In short order, we walked home in full-on argument mode once again. He didn't cool off before we reached our house. We assumed the girls were in bed asleep.

Once inside, behind the covered windows and in the privacy of our home, Chris went berserk. He turned violent, chasing me around the house. I knew if he caught me it wouldn't end well. I ran into our fourth bedroom, which we used as an office, and locked the door. Chris banged on the door, punching it and kicking it. His rage was so powerful that he put a hole through the door.

Savannah raced out of her room. She yelled at Madison, who had opened her door when awakened by the ruckus, to go back inside her room, shut her door, and lock it. Savannah ran up to Chris, still trying to kick down the office door. I curled up on the floor, afraid. Chris hurled obscenities at me.

Savannah, a college athlete, strong and strong-willed, grabbed her father and pushed him against the wall. He was drunk and not able to gain an upper hand against her. When he tried to fight back, Savannah threw him against the wall again, and he crumpled to the ground. She ran and gathered up all the keys in the house so he couldn't drive away.

"I've had enough of you!" she yelled at Chris.

Chris eventually passed out, while I remained locked in the room for hours, lying in the middle of the floor, the scent of carpet cleaning tingling my nose, unable to look at Chris or even face Savannah. I felt so many things: shame, exhaustion, and fear. I wondered where we'd go from here.

A few days later, January 7, was Savannah's last day of winter break before she returned to college. I wanted to do something as a family before she left, so I convinced everyone to play another board game. Savannah had no interest, but I coaxed her into it, saying it would be a fun activity to do on her last day. Thankfully, there were no issues, and we all enjoyed the game. It was a sweet time.

It was the last day Savannah would ever spend with Chris.

When Savannah arrived back at college, we spoke on the phone. I had been wondering if she would say anything about the last few weeks of conflict with Chris.

"Mom, you can't keep doing this with Dad," she began. Instant sadness wrapped around my heart. *No daughter should need to protect her mother at this stage in life.* "He's too much. You're going to get hurt. Someone else needs to handle him because you can't anymore. He's out of control." Her words tumbled out in rapid-fire succession. I had little to say as a rebuttal. Both proud of her maturity and filled with sorrow for how fast she had to grow up, I mumbled in agreement.

The thirty days were up, and Chris and I hadn't discussed anything about the last month, our marriage, or plans for divorce yet.

———

January 9, 2015: Daytime

Hail and Farewell ceremonies in the military celebrate changes in command at the director and senior officer levels. Full of pomp and circumstance, they honor those who are departing and welcome those who are joining the base, introducing them to the culture and traditions of their new organization.

There are no official requirements outlined by the United States Military to have a Hail and Farewell celebration, though it is common. It is up to each unit to carry out this tradition as it sees fit. The United States Navy, on the other hand, employs a specific custom that officers must host a formal dinner when new leaders arrive. It is very much a social celebration, at least at GTMO. I had attended many of these ceremonies over the four years we had been on base.

When I was promoted to director of the Fleet and Family Support Center, as a department head, I had a Hail and Farewell ceremony. Chris had never been a fan of them; as a civilian, he had rarely received a formal invite. Sometimes, he attended as my "plus one" since I held the department head position. Other times, he declined to go at all. There were some occasions when he did receive a personal invite to a Hail and Farewell if the departing senior officer was a friend of his.

Traditionally, people join their spouses on stage if they are introduced during the ceremony. Chris did not come up with me during my Hail and Farewell. He believed being my "plus one" was a slap in the face and that he deserved better.

This particular Hail and Farewell was for the change of command at the XO position, or the second-in-command/executive officer. Since Chris had a professional and friendly relationship with the departing XO, he received his own formal invitation and was excited to attend, believing he had every right to be there.

The day started out perfectly. With Chris in an amiable mood, we made plans to have lunch with Kelly and another friend, Randy, who was the head of Personnel Support Detachment (PSD). Stateside, Civilians are not permitted to eat at The Galley, but at GTMO, with few alternative options available, we were allowed to eat there, and we thoroughly enjoyed Surf and Turf Day at The Galley on base. It wasn't often we had lobster for lunch, and everyone was in a good mood. Conversation flowed between the four of us.

Chris and I had taken half-days off from work in preparation for the Hail and Farewell that evening. When we arrived home after lunch, we called Savannah via FaceTime. Again, our conversation with her was lighthearted and positive. Looking back, I'm grateful for this time. Savannah's last communication with Chris would be a special memory, an upbeat FaceTime call, rather than the memory of his rampage in our home, filled with anger, fear, and distrust.

As we moved through the afternoon, we reminded Madison about our family rule. If we were going out, she had to solidify any plans with her friends ahead of time. We weren't going to be gone and have her texting or calling about where she was going or have us wondering where she was. While GTMO was one of the safest places to live, we had raised our teenagers with the mindset that one day, we'd be back in the States. We felt getting into the habit of telling us where they were going and having a curfew and using the "buddy system" at all times was a wise parenting practice.

Madison's plans for the night were still up in the air as we approached the time we had to leave for the Hail and Farewell ceremony. So, she stayed home for the night. We had satellite cable and the Internet. We lived in a neighborhood with the families of senior chiefs on base and even some of her friends lived on our street. We didn't think twice about leaving her home alone for the night as a first-year high schooler.

Around 6:00 p.m., I was on the phone with Kelly. We were going to pick her up on the way to the Officers' Club, and I wanted to give her a few-minute warning so she could be ready to go. While on the phone, Chris suggested the two of us do a pre-party shot together. He abstained since he was driving, but he made me a "Buttery Nipple," and Kelly and I downed our shots while on the phone, before we headed out the door. Our fabulous day continued.

My heart swelled with everyone's good mood, especially Chris's. I knew it was either feast or famine with him, soaring highs of adventure or dark lows of violence and envy. This day seemed to be blessed with Fun Chris. At this point, I don't think I was in love with Chris anymore, but I thought of him more as a friend. When he was soaring, any day of our twenty-year marriage, I enjoyed his company. We knew how to have fun together. When we were good, we were good. Unfortunately, those times had been few and far between.

On the way to the Officers' Club, Kelly mentioned taking pictures of the event for the base's weekly newspaper. Fleetingly, I found that odd. She had never brought a camera before. But it meant she had a bag with her. I never carried a purse, so I dropped my Blackberry in her bag, knowing Chris had his flip phone on him, in his pocket, should Madison need to get a hold of us.

When we arrived, we first went to the upstairs bar to grab a round of drinks. Each of us ordered, and as I looked around, I didn't see many people. We didn't stay upstairs long. The Hail and Farewell party was held downstairs in what was called the Hangar Bar. It was dismal down there, and I was surprised this was the location for this event. They had cleaned up the space, but it reminded me of my parents' basement, complete with folding tables and drab music playing from the speakers. It was about as big as a residential basement, too. As guests arrived, we eventually stood elbow-to-elbow. This was no swanky bar.

I briefly thought, "Why would you want to take pictures of this?"

By 6:30 p.m., it seemed everyone was drinking. Socializing had begun, and we all waited for the official start to the Hail and Farewell Ceremony.

CHAPTER 14
A NIGHT OF ASSAULTS

"People forget that there's two sides to every story. Of course somebody is going to tell the side of it that makes them look good and exaggerate the rest to make everyone else look bad."
—David Reeves

By now, age thirty-nine, I had spent nearly twenty years with a spouse who had convinced me that I was ugly, stupid, and lazy. During one vacation, I stood in front of a full-length mirror, and Chris walked into the room.

"You know, I've gotten used to the way you look," he said, "but if you wanted to change a few things, I wouldn't be opposed to it . . . now that we have some money."

His words pierced my already fragile self-image and would affect me for years to come, causing me to seek out a plastic surgeon. Of course, the surgeon couldn't fix my issues with body-image; they weren't rooted in anything physical. It would be a slow mental and emotional healing process that would last for years.

Through the past several years, a number of people had witnessed Chris's verbal, emotional, and physical abuse toward me. They had seen him slap me in the face, slam my fingers in doors, pull my hair, and choke me. People had picked him up to avoid police intervention, yanked him off me and slammed him into walls to get him to stop hurting me, and peered at the holes in our furniture and walls.

Chris's response was always, "I'm just joking," or "It's no big deal." Or, he'd hide behind the childish and victim-mentality response of "I'm going to kill myself" so people wouldn't think the worst of him. They viewed him as a victim, too. He was a showman. The power and control he had created over me was honed with those who knew of his violence, keeping them from doing anything about it but short-term rescues. I don't blame them. Look at how long I had done the same thing.

I lived in two different worlds every day. The world at work and the world at home. And I had been groomed by the years of abuse to feel and think differently at each place. Chris had always told me everything was my fault. If I would have behaved better, he wouldn't have to do what he did or talk to me the way he did. The name-calling left an indelible mark on my soul. Over the years, much like victims of abduction who no longer try to escape, but accept their prison, I embraced my life. I felt every bit as ugly as he said I was. I felt worthless, as though no one would ever love me for me. I believed I was stupid. Chris used to tell me I was the "smartest dumbest person he had ever met."

Today, when I think of that woman, the one who just several short years ago, bought into those lies, my heart breaks. I wasn't just a caged animal. He had convinced me I was trash. A weak woman . . . And so I was.

At work, however, I felt skilled, important, and capable. My work reviews, the feedback I received—including when I was in school for my doctoral degrees—and my promotions communicated to me that I was smart and successful.

When I walked in the office each day, I entered an emotional sanctuary of sorts. I thought I could do anything. I loved going to work (or school in the years before GTMO) because when I was working or learning, I felt smart and strong. I had staff under me who trusted me and respected me. When it came to the families and clients we served, I never wanted anybody to feel like I did at home. That's why I had chosen my particular field—family services. I thrived with helping others and believed I could make changes. And when I encountered abusive relationships, I did everything I could to help or problem-solve. When I worked late, it wasn't because I was getting into trouble. I was writing new curriculum and desperately seeking ways to help people like me. People trapped in domestic prisons—angry, depressed, abused, or otherwise unsatisfied—caged spouses who had nowhere to turn. But often, I felt deflated as I ran into the brick wall that is government bureaucracy. The dreaded red tape.

Still, I believed that someday, I would find my way out if I could find a way out for others. After all, I had climbed from education specials to director. Maybe I could work hard enough that I could fix this systemic problem, too. My job meant everything to me, and I didn't want anyone else to live the way I had been living for twenty years. I just couldn't figure out a way to be smart and strong at home. I relied heavily on Kristie, the domestic violence advocate at the Fleet and Family Support Center, gravitating to her for both professional and personal reasons. I drank in her ideas; they were as much for my work responsibilities as they were for my home life. I desperately wanted to confide in her, but I was her superior. It felt awkward, maybe even wrong.

––––––––––

January 9, 2015: Evening

> *I have given my account of this night countless times over the years. No matter how many times I talk about January 9 and January 10, the stories from people who were also intoxicated, who held no significance in our lives, who saw only small snippets of the events, or who didn't know our story at all seem to take precedence over mine and those who were close to us. Most people point and say it was all about me or the CO and me or even Chris and me—the latter being closer to the truth. Two-thirds of those stories, the most public ones until now, are opinions, and honestly, their perspectives don't matter.*
>
> *For years, I've kept silent. It's my turn now. I hope you'll read this account with an open mind, especially now that you know the backstory, the authentic condition of my marriage, our home life, and the cage I lived in for twenty years.*

When we made it to the lower bar at the Hail and Farewell, Chris and I ordered another round of our signature drinks: a Captain and coke for him and a Jamison and coke for me. The tall glasses from the upstairs bar gave way to small cups standing no more than four inches high in this basement bar.

My mom had taught me in my first year of college, back at age eighteen, to "never accept an open container and never leave your drink and come back to it and drink it." It was advice I had lived by for two decades. If I ordered a drink, sipped some, set it down, and walked away, even for a minute or two, I simply went back to the bar to get another.

Drinks were cheap at GTMO. We could afford to order another even if we hadn't finished the previous one.

On the outside, it appears I am downing alcohol like nobody's business. It's a small detail, but it's important to me.

Everyone was drinking but had kept it respectable since the ceremony was about to begin.

Because this Hail and Farewell was only for the incoming and outgoing XOs, it was a private party. The guest list was specific—an intimate group of department heads and senior officers. There were a few senior enlisted members who had come, as well. While it was a social evening, I stood among peers and authority figures. It was nice to see people apart from our ultra-professional work environment. Gifts were exchanged, and we waited for the ceremony to start, where speeches would take up a good portion of the night.

The outgoing XO speeches came first, and I smiled as I listened to all the people who had been impacted by him. This particular XO had been, in essence, my mentor. Known as a good person, he was also blunt, and I enjoyed his colorful Navy stories. He and the business manager had been the influencers who had paved the way for me to take the role of director. I could have given a speech, but I elected to thank him privately.

While I was used to the stage in my work, teaching groups of 500 people or more and giving speeches in other arenas, I wanted my gratitude for his mentorship of me to be personal. So that's what I did. I pulled him aside before he departed for the evening, knowing I'd likely not see him again. I thanked him for my career and told him he was a huge part of my success. Then the XO left.

The incoming XO received his welcome, and the evening turned solely social. Chris and I and those whom we were with drank some more. We shared shots with the CO and with the incoming XO. J.R. mentioned having people over to his house after the Hail and Farewell ended. Chris and I nodded. Throughout the evening, sometimes, Chris and I were together. Other times we mingled with different people. It was fun for quite a while.

Then—the moment that changed everything. I was enjoying a casual, side conversation with a friend, Tara. She was the head of the Morale Welfare and Recreation Department (MWR). It was just girl talk, nothing of significance. Chris, unable to leave me alone to have privacy for long, walked up to us and attempted to insert himself in our intimate discussion. I had become less tolerant of him doing this, and I put up my hand. This wasn't the first time, nor even the hundredth time, Chris had tried to break up a conversation between me and someone else.

One time, he had disrupted a girls' night at the Officers' Club where friends and I were singing karaoke. Other times, he would call me while I was out, begging me to come home because he was sick and needed help.

"No. Go away," I said with my hand up, stopping him in his tracks. "We're having our own conversation."

Still at the height of his paranoia, he didn't like being shut out of anything, no matter how inconsequential it was. This act set him off. Instantly, his irritation showed as his eyes narrowed. He looked like a wounded child.

Irritation morphed into rage, and he stormed off. I don't know where he went, but I didn't see him for some time. I finished chatting with Tara, never guessing it was a big deal. I moved around the room, speaking with others, including a few of the pilots. We talked about how I hated flying and all wondered why. Then, I went over to the corner of the bar where J.R. was sitting. I grabbed the stool around the side of the bar, so we weren't sitting next to each other.

Others would later tell the story of how I was barely dressed, how I was dancing and throwing myself on him. They make it sound like I had grabbed a pole on top of the bar and let loose. Those stories are crazy. And they couldn't be further from the truth. While I was intoxicated, I was fully clothed in ceremony-appropriate attire. At most, our elbows were touching because we sat on each corner of the bar while he chatted. Because of the noise level, me and every other person having a conversation there, leaned toward their friends' faces so we could hear the other person. I wasn't whispering in his ear, nor was he in mine.

Yes, we had been involved in an "entanglement" in Jacksonville, and yes, we were good friends at this point and knew a lot about each other. But we were sitting among thirty of my peers and his subordinates. I don't care how drunk two people would have to be to do anything in that environment, but I was in complete charge of my faculties. I was aware of everything. We weren't kissing. We were not doing anything wrong.

J.R. reiterated that he was having people over to his house later. He never personally invited me, but I said, "Okay," and then, "I don't know" in response.

I knew I was reaching the point of drunkenness that meant I should head home soon. My friends could attest to the fact that I always go home to lay down after drinking, always wanting to remain in control while out. I never wanted to jeopardize my career or my ability to help others in my job. When I had had enough alcohol, I knew it, and I was close at this point.

As J.R. and I ended our conversation, and I stood up to walk away, Chris approached and said he wanted to talk to me outside.

"Fine," I said and followed him up the four steps beside the bar to the alleyway where people smoked. No one else was there. Chris turned around and grabbed me, yelling at me and then pushing me against the wall. Terror erupted in my gut. There was nowhere to run. I tried to push him off me, and he screamed, "What the (explicative) is wrong with you? Don't you want to be married?"

The thirty days had passed. "No!" I yelled. "No, Chris! We're done. Get your hands off me!" I raised my voice even louder, hoping someone would hear me. "Get the (explicative) away from me!" Afraid of what Chris might do, I just wanted us to be somewhere safe. I wanted to stop feeling afraid all the time. I wanted to be back inside. "I don't want to be married anymore!"

I maneuvered away from him, panicked because he had reached the level of violence he had shown when he was banging and kicking our office door at home—the time Savannah had been prompted to intervene. I knew what to expect next, so I wanted to put as much distance between us as possible.

I raced down the steps and back into the Hangar Bar. People had started to leave, making their way toward the atrium in Bayview that separated the restaurant from the Officers' Club. My goal was to find Kelly. I knew he'd come after me, but I slowed down, so as not to draw too much attention to myself. I went up the front stairs and to the front of the mass of people who were walking outside, just trying to locate Kelly.

Once outside, I turned and faced the building. To my left was Officers' Circle, the street on which upper-level officers lived. J.R.'s house was at the end. I remembered him saying he was having people over. To my right was a bus stop. Behind me was the parking lot, where some people were finding their cars, despite the legal driving limit on base being .05.

As I stood outside, looking around for my friends, Chris burst through the front doors. His aggressive movements paled in comparison to his verbal tirade. He spied me on the road.

Over the past two decades, I had learned to shut down when Chris screamed at me. His voice would sound muffled and far away, much like the teacher in the *Charlie Brown* comic strip. Except this was anything but funny. I think over time, my emotional brain recognized I couldn't listen to the words he hurled at me. In public, when he would attack me with his insults, I learned to stop arguing. Maybe it was a coping mechanism. Maybe it was self-defense. I don't know. Chris had also learned something. In this abusive dance between the two of us, he understood he could use my smallness and stillness against me. His name-calling increased.

That night, my ears turned off, just as they had dozens of times before. I heard pieces of his attack. A few words here and there. "Whore . . . his (explicative) must be big . . ."

While I shrank away in self-protection, I still felt things. My gut twisted with shame. In my peripheral vision, I noticed people had stopped to stare at us. I wanted to disappear. I prayed I really was shrinking, moving far out of sight . . . I hoped forever.

Numb, cheeks red and hot, I stood frozen. Chris was nearly upon me, and he raised his fist as if to punch me in the face. Time slowed. In the next moment, a few people grabbed him. J.R. stood between us. Once Chris was contained in the hands of others, the new XO told J.R. to go home, that he would handle it. I saw my opportunity to get away and started to follow him, thinking of the people who would be at his house for the after party—protection, in my quick assessment. I didn't know the party at J.R.'s house had been cancelled.

The new XO grabbed me.

"Stop chasing the CO!" he told me.

"I'm not! I'm trying to get away from my husband," I gasped.

"I know exactly what's happening," he continued. "Stop pining for the CO and stay away from him."

I balked. "My husband is a lunatic," I explained. "He assaulted me once earlier and just tried to do it again. I'm asking for help!"

The XO's response: "Then maybe you need to divorce him."

I felt as if he had slapped me in the face. His words were flippant, arrogant.

"I'm asking for help!" I begged.

The XO turned and ordered Chris to go home, home to our fourteen-year-old daughter. He was in no condition to be home alone with her. But I didn't feel like I could protest. He wasn't listening to my pleas for help. I had been dismissed.

The XO then ordered me to go home with Kelly. Like a pat on a dog's head, the XO felt he had handled the situation. He hadn't . . .

Kelly ushered me back inside where we took refuge in the ladies' room.

Tears threatened despite the shock of the events. A sob caught in my throat. I couldn't believe he had caused such a public debacle. Kelly had seen Chris go berserk before when he had pushed in the door to her house and chased me under a table. She had been part of the searches when Chris had gone missing for a night, and she had read some of his vulgar and threatening text messages over the years.

We decided to wait it out in the bathroom. I sat on the couch in the lounge area while Kelly took a minute to enter a stall. Within another minute or two, Chris came barreling into the women's bathroom. He pinned me on the couch, screaming obscenities. Snapping out of shock, I thought, "This is it."

Kelly tore out of the stall and managed to push him out of the restroom. She locked the door and turned to face me. We gasped for our breaths. We heard plates crashing to the floor outside the bathroom and looked at each other, eyes wide. I wondered where the XO was now. Chris had thoroughly lost it. We stayed put until there had been a considerable amount of silence, hopeful Chris had finally left.

That was the last time I ever saw Chris.

––––––––––

My account of this night has never wavered since 2015 because it's the truth. Others have changed their stories. On one hand, I wish no one had stepped in on the street outside the Officers' Club. I wish Chris would have punched me in the face so that there was proof of the events that transpired. Witness testimony can be so tricky. I wish Kelly hadn't stopped him from hurting me in the bathroom. Because then there'd be proof. The behavior some people described just wasn't in line with Chris's character or MO. The words they said he yelled weren't words he would ever have used. I wish my small posturing to protect myself didn't happen. The content of the trials and interviews that commenced after the night of January 9, 2015 were not only mind-boggling, but frustrating.

Kelly and I opened the door of the restroom and peered out. Chris was nowhere in sight. I moved over to the atrium sitting area and plopped down. Kelly left and walked through the Officers' Club to call for a safe ride for us. I was exhausted. I sat and stared straight ahead, trying to make sense of everything that had just happened. A woman went in and then came out of the restroom. Spying me still sitting there, she asked, "Are you okay?"

"I'm fine," I smiled in reply. I was anything but fine.

Kelly and the new XO arrived and said our safe ride was waiting outside. I eyed the XO suspiciously. When he had ignored my pleas for help, he had allowed Chris to come back for me in the restroom. *Thanks for your help,* I thought angrily.

Later, the XO would testify that he went back inside to make sure I was okay. But if he had, he would have either seen Chris before he entered the bathroom or seen him chucking plates to the floor once Kelly had locked the door. The reason Chris was able to enter that building again was because the XO was already back at the tiki bar having a drink. He would also later testify he only had two beers that night. That too, was a lie under oath. He had done a shot with Chris and me and others earlier that evening. He had been drinking with everyone else. He had ignored my request for help after I explained Chris had assaulted me earlier that night and had tried again in front of other witnesses on the street. In January 2020, a defense team would end up calling him a liar in the courtroom . . . because he was.

Once at Kelly's house, fear and anger gave way to exhaustion. I assumed Chris was home with Madison, sleeping off his drunken rage. I slept on Kelly's couch. When I woke up, I felt like I was drowning, feeling so sick. I had never felt that way before. Anger returned. "Why am I the one on someone else's couch when Chris is the one who attacked me?" I had done nothing wrong that night. I had simply put up a hand to block Chris from interrupting a conversation between a friend and me and then told him I didn't want to be married to him anymore in that alleyway. That's all I did.

CHAPTER 15

MISSING

"Has he ever trapped you in a room and not let you out? Has he ever raised a fist as if he were going to hit you? Has he ever thrown an object that hit you or nearly did? Has he ever held you down or grabbed you to restrain you? Has he ever shoved, poked, or grabbed you? Has he ever threatened to hurt you? If the answer to any of these questions is yes, then we can stop wondering whether he'll ever be violent; he already has been."
—**Lundy Bancroft** in *Why Does He Do That?: Inside the Minds of Angry and Controlling Men*

January 10, 2015

I am awake and feeling sick. Kelly approaches me and asks if I want anything to eat. She's heading to McDonald's with Randy, the department head for Personnel Safety Detachment. The three of us work together often, and he had been the friend who ate with us at The Galley.

The thought of food doesn't make me feel better, so I decline.

"Okay," says Kelly. "We'll be back."

I think it's odd that Kelly doesn't say anything about the previous night. I figure we'll talk about it at some point. I'm actually grateful. I'm not ready to discuss it. I also realize she never took any photos during the Hail and Farewell. I briefly think that's for the best. Everyone was drunk.

I stand up and walk around her house, thinking about my next move. I know I have to figure out a different home situation. I can't go back there. I am worried about what Chris might do. I hope Madison is okay and then assume she'd have called if she needed help.

A little while later, Kelly and Randy return but without food. Briefly, my gut tells me something is off. *Maybe they ate it on the way home.*

"Hey, Lara, aren't you worried about where Chris is?" they ask me.

"He's home," I say, now with less conviction. *Isn't he?*

"He's not home," Kelly says. "We just came from there, and he's nowhere to be found." As she's speaking, irritation bubbles to the surface. I feel betrayed that they would go to my house without me. Then, my mind quickly shifts to Madison. *She's been home alone!*

I scramble out of Kelly's house and into her car. I hold concern for my daughter but not for Chris. I assume he's off on another one of his childish escapades. As we head home, anger spikes as I look into the woods to see if I can see him hiding. That's where he was the last time he had done this—spying on me.

With Kelly in tow, we rush through my front door and call for Madison. I hurl silent questions and accusations at Kelly. *Why would you ask me if I was worried? You know Chris has done this before! You've been the one to help me look for him!*

Madison is okay, safe and sound in bed. It's still fairly early. I jump into the shower, anxious to rid myself of the memories of last night. I notice finger-shaped bruises on my upper arm. Moving to my bed, I lie down, overwhelmed. Madi asks me why we never came home. I explain our fight to her. I'm honest with my daughter, sharing I had been told to stay at Kelly's house and her dad was supposed to be here. We assume, together, he had decided to run off again.

"Where did he go, Mom," she asks.

"I don't know, but he'll be back soon."

Kelly and Randy have left. When I emerge from the bedroom, Kelly calls and confides in me that she spoke to Chris last night on the phone while we were waiting for the safe ride.

"He was so angry," she says to me.

"I bet," I reply.

"I told him to go home." I nod in reply, even though she can't see me.

That's the end of the conversation. I have nothing else to say about Chris, and I assume she doesn't either. He should be here, and my jaw clenches as we all have to take time, again, to look for him. Kelly and Randy come back to pick me up so we can drive around looking for Chris.

Just as we did back in October, we travel our normal route, looking for Chris. I have already checked my backyard, so we hit the marina. We look on the boat. We go to any place we know he's run to in the past. No luck.

It's nearly noon, so we decide to let J.R. know that Chris is still missing. I'm feeling apathetic to everything. Chris has trained me not to worry about him after a drunken fiasco when he hasn't returned home. Last night, he made a fool of himself. Everyone on base likely knows about his tirade. I'm sure he's hiding somewhere, trying to figure out what to do next—how to manage his situation and his reputation to make himself look better.

Kelly, Randy, and I arrive at J.R.'s office. It's large with a window view of the bay. He's sitting behind his desk, in front of the dark wood paneling on the back wall. Historical paintings and medals fill the other walls—a manly kind of office, yet proud . . . Navy proud. There is a private bathroom off to the side. I take a seat directly in front of J.R., Kelly sits beside me, and Randy sits by the door. I am not desperate to find Chris. I don't think anything about my behavior or attitude is wrong, but I can feel the weight of a thousand embarrassments and failures. Everyone in this room knows Chris disappears often, so I'm not sure what to say, but I start the conversation:

"I'm done. I don't want Chris to come back to our house. Find him another house. I can't be under the same roof as him again . . . neither can Madison." Chris had trampled on my public, professional life, and I will never forget it. I look at J.R. pointedly. "Or find Madison and me another house. I need sponsorship." I am afraid. I know this is a tipping point.

"After last night, I also want to file formal domestic violence charges," I continue. The words are just tumbling out, but I don't care. "I am absolutely done." I feel the tingling of tears in the creases of my eyes. Just the memory of Chris grabbing my arm in the alleyway and raising his fist to punch me . . . of him tackling me on the couch in the bathroom . . . I want to be clear with everyone in that room that I am not taking it anymore. I am done being a victim.

No one says anything for a beat. Then, J.R. asks about the places Chris might be hiding. We fill him in on all the locations we've already checked and any others where he might be lying low.

"He has his phone and cards and keys on him," I offer. As the manager of Navy Exchange Loss Prevention, he has keys to numerous places. "You know, he can sustain himself for a while," I say. *And it won't be the first time he does*, I think.

"I'm so angry." I know I'm repeating myself. I want them to know this isn't going to be like the previous times when I took him back. "He's made our private situation public!" My heart is racing. I want to hold it together, so I breathe in deeply. I hate that Chris has control again. He's controlling our lives this very moment, and I can't follow through on my intentions to leave him when he's hiding.

J.R. starts a base-wide search, involving multiple parties and agencies. I still don't understand what the big deal is, but he and Kelly keep me in the loop as the day wears on and no one finds Chris.

Since Chris had been scoping out our house in October and had threatened me, the decision is made to put patrols on our street and in front of our house. My domestic violence advocate, Kristie, arrives to keep me company. I didn't want to be alone, so she takes off her "direct report" hat and puts on her "domestic violence advocate" hat for me. I am afraid of what Chris might do if he gets into the house at this point.

We talk and I learn Kristie has wondered about our home life for months. Chris's behavior had spilled over into the public eye at times before last night, and while I suspect others could figure out what's been going on under our roof, she is the only one doing and saying something about it. Kristie is brilliant, and I am thankful for her, both in this moment and as one of my staff members. I wish I had confided in her sooner.

I tell Madison that her dad is officially missing. I can't hide it. CID, the military's version of crime scene investigators, come and go. During the course of their investigation, they take my statement about last evening's events and what I know—which is not much.

I can't seem to rest. As the hours tick by, I start to feel worried. Chris has threatened suicide to get what he wanted before. I wonder where he could be.

I call Savannah to tell her that her father is missing. Her reaction parallels mine. "He can't come back home, Mom. He needs help! You have to be done with this. When they find him, he needs help, somewhere away from GTMO . . . like professional help," she says with force. I nod my head, again knowing the person on the other side of the line can't see me. I am ashamed my daughter has to be the one to say all these things to me, but I know she's right.

"Right now, we just need to know where he is," I reply without energy.

My next phone call is to my parents. I tell them Chris has been missing and share all the details of last night. They express sadness but no surprise. Though an ocean and thousands of miles away, they offer whatever support I need.

As I call Chris's mom, I feel emotionally exhausted. I explain the basics: He was drunk last night. He ran off. We can't find him. As she listens, she becomes frustrated. I know she's thinking about the last time she saw him in August. The weekend he wanted to go to Las Vegas while we were stateside, dropping Savannah off at college for the first time— the time she took my side. I'm sure his f-word-loaded retort is ringing in her ears. She has seen his aggression. She is not surprised by anything I say, either.

It's now evening, and everyone at GTMO knows Chris Tur is missing, and I feel shattered. Split wide open with everyone's opinions, advice, and gossip. As a private person, I want to run away and hide, too. The whole day has been surreal.

With darkness, the teams call off the door-to-door search. My fear escalates. I rub my arms to calm the shiver, though the air is not cold. *What if Chris is waiting for the cover of night to come here?* I fear for my life.

Kristie agrees to stay with me overnight. I cannot bring myself to sleep in our bedroom, to lie in Chris's and my bed, so the two of us take the couches in the living room. Madison is in her bed. I don't sleep but rather toss and turn all night.

CHAPTER 16

THE WEIGHT OF SADNESS (PART 2)

"There is a sacredness in tears. They are not the mark of weakness but of power. They speak more eloquently than ten thousand tongues."
—Washington Irving

January 11, 2015

My anger has ebbed. It's Sunday morning, and the base-wide search has come up empty. No Chris. No answers. I don't feel good about this now.

The phone rings, and NCIS is on the other end.

"Mrs. Tur, can you come help us out with the search?" Walter Bulnes's voice seems stern on the other end of the phone.

I agree to go into their offices.

A couple of hours of "interrogation" in a white-walled room pass. I move between disbelief and frustration as NCIS agents ask me questions. *How is this helping the search?* Then, I'm suddenly ushered to a conference room. As I enter, my stomach drops, and I raise my hand to my mouth. I know my life will be forever altered.

"I'm so sorry, but we found your husband's body this morning—" the CO says, as I stand in a room filled with people in full military dress.

Sagging into a nearby chair, sobs erupt from my throat, and all I can feel is immense sadness. All of my physical senses go numb. My peripheral vision evaporates, but it doesn't matter. Tears block my vision. I hear others speak, but their muffled voices offer no solace: "I'm sorry."

Minutes later, as I walk out of the building alongside the chaplain, who has been tasked with driving me home, I wonder what words I can possibly say to Madi . . . and to Savannah. Their father is gone. I catch and stuff another sob. I can only focus on one minute at a time.

The chaplain drives Chris's red Jeep, and I sit in the passenger seat, frozen in time. I see the other houses on the street as we head toward ours, but their once vibrant colors are muted. *Dead?* Even the word sounds so final.

I climb out of the Jeep and shuffle toward the front door. Before I realize it, Madison is standing before me. I open my mouth, but the look of anguish on her face as her eyes close and her lips form a flat line, tells me she already knows what I'm about to say. Later, I would learn she knew the minute she realized it wasn't Chris driving his Jeep. I think, "She's only fourteen," and my mama's heart tears. I know this day is a mark of trauma my daughters will never forget. In my mind's eye, I see so many possibilities wilt with the news I share with her. *Graduation day without a dad. No father-daughter wedding dance. The pride of showing a grandfather his grandchild, all gone.*

"Madi . . . your dad is dead. He's passed away," I finally say. I can't look at her without releasing my stuffed sob. The chaplain comforts us with kind words, most of which I don't hear. I only remember the tone of his voice, calm and soothing.

I know I have to get in touch with Savannah. I also know this isn't information I can just tell her over the phone. *I can't believe I won't be with her to hug her when I tell her.* I need someone I trust to be with her, to stand in my place. She can't hear this alone. I call Amy, their godmother and my long-time friend. She lives near Savannah's college campus. She has always been a part of their lives. Sometimes, the girls have called Amy their "other mother," and now, I find solace in that. She's the one.

I dial, hands shaking with dread.

"Hey!" Amy's voice slides through the phone, and I feel an ounce of relief. *Thank goodness—she answered.* I take a deep breath.

"Amy, I need you to go find Savannah," I say. I hear the fragility in my voice. "I need to tell her something, and I need you to stay with her. Don't let her out of your sight."

"Okay. Yup," she replies and asks no further questions. She can hear the anguish, too. I love her for that discretion. The first two people who need to know about Chris are his daughters. I can't tell anyone else before them.

Amy calls Savannah and tells her I need something from her. She asks her to meet her at a specific location on campus so she can pick her up. Once Amy is with Savannah, sitting in her car, I talk to my oldest daughter:

"Savannah, they found your dad." I pause. "He's dead, honey," I say. I pinch the bridge of my nose. For a quick second, there is silence. Then, I hear a *bang*.

"Hello?"

Amy's voice answers. "She just threw the phone and took off! I'm going after her. What did you say to her?"

"I just told her that Chris is dead," I say. "Please stay with her," I beg Amy. My heart breaks into pieces I could never count because I cannot be there with her right now. A mother's worst nightmare.

Amy takes off running, no match for an eighteen-year-old athlete. She sees Savannah run into her dorm, and with the security measures in place, Amy can't follow. She stands outside the dormitory, worried, and pacing. A few minutes later, Savannah re-emerges. She carries a necklace and a letter—things Chris had sent her.

"I just needed to get these," she says to Amy. Then, Savannah breaks down and cries.

I talk with Savannah for a bit. We console each other. I know she's holding things back. A mother's intuition. Later, things will bubble up to the surface. They always do.

CHAPTER 17

GRIEF

"Don't sacrifice yourself too much because if you sacrifice too much, there's nothing else you can give and nobody will care for you."
—**Karl Lagerfeld**

The day is a blur. One child is with me, and the other is too far away for a mother's heart to tolerate. They are the first and second people on my mind and will be all day. All week. Forever. But as thoughts come and go in rapid-fire succession, I know I have to notify the rest of our family.

First, however, Madison and I sit with the chaplain. What a blessing he is. We pray and talk about life and death and what we want to do. We want to have a service here, in GTMO. Our home has been this base for the past four years, so I want the funeral to be here. Even when Chris and I had lived stateside, we hadn't built many relationships with people, and our closest friends not associated with GTMO are back from our childhood or shortly after getting married. Most of our friends, those we call family, are here. I reason Dawnell and Mark can travel back.

I feel a measure of peace after spending a short time with the chaplain, and I know it's time to make some calls, the calls no one ever wants to receive. I start with my parents. In grief, I believe we turn to those we know the best and the longest. We race to those who have watched us grow up. I am no different. In these moments, I just want my mom.

My parents ask if they and my brother can come down. I think for a second and decline their offer. There are so many people here already. The base is full of friends, a family-like community. It's the double-edged sword that is GTMO. The bad part is the gossip and lack of privacy. In times of utter joy, such as births of babies and the renewals of vows, we celebrate. And in the deepest sorrows, we mourn together as a close-knit group. In good times and bad, people become suctioned to each other. I know I won't be alone, even if I want to be. I decide the only people who should probably come down are Savannah, certainly, and Chris's brothers.

Next, I call Chris's mom. I struggle internally as I dial. I know the last time Ann saw Chris, he had been aggressive with her. But she's also his mom. They loved each other, even if they had their own way of showing it. I cannot imagine what the words I'm about to say will do to her heart. I push that thought out of my mind, or I won't be able to speak.

Ann is understandably devastated. When she asks about traveling down, I make the recommendation that she stay home. I say it may be best if just Mike and Hank come. They have never visited in the four years we have lived here. I believe this is the right thing to do right now.

I know I won't be able to take care of my girls, myself, and Chris's mom. Selfishly, my decision is solely about me—a form of self-care, something I have struggled with for the past twenty years. It's time I stand up for what I need.

Later, I'd learn I'd offended Ann and the family. I understand. I do. However, in this moment and for the week ahead, my hazy thoughts and the feeling of the ground swallowing me up allow me to only focus on Madison, Savannah, and myself. I want to do what's best for the three of us; I want to grieve with my GTMO family. Right now, that means saying no to Chris's mom, my parents, and my brother. It's every bit a personal decision, not an exclusionary one.

You can't care for Ann, too.
Chris is your husband. This is your home.
These are your daughters.
You can't do this. You can't have everyone here.

These thoughts fly through my head, leaving a trail of despair. I won't realize until much later that asking Ann to stay stateside is so offensive. I don't know this will cause another fight within his family as they rail against me. But I just can't do it.

There is a small piece of my heart unable to feel the burden of Chris's and my last moments together. The violence. The emotional end of our marriage. My readiness to move on, and his anger that left the bruises on my arm. Now his death. The end has happened in the most undesirable way, the most public way, and it hasn't even become that public yet. I could never fathom what is about to transpire in the weeks and even months to come.

I hang up the phone. It's hard to breathe. I know my parents feel helpless, and Chris's mom wants to be here, but I can't think about these things right now. Others are making arrangements. I should be a part of that, even though I'm in a stupor that I can't escape. *Is this really happening?*

In the next minute, I know I have to pull it together for my kids. I talk to Kelly, and she scrambles to finalize the orders to get Savannah and Chris's brothers on the next flight to Cuba. I start to plan Chris's service with those who have stopped by the house to help me, particularly the chaplain. We decide on the following Saturday as the date, which will give enough time for people to arrive, to plan the repass—or wake as some people call it—and plan the dinner for after the service. I vaguely hear someone mention an obituary. Later, one would be posted in the base's newspaper. The number of moving parts is overwhelming. I can sense my brain shutting down and my heart turning numb.

As the day moves ahead, people bring food—casseroles begin to fill my refrigerator and freezer. They aren't the only people who come by. NCIS is interviewing people, despite everyone's state of mourning. I just sit there, on a chair in my house, and think about Chris. A little. Mostly, I think about Madison and Savannah. I don't think about much else.

After some time, as I've done in the past, I become mechanical, paste on a smile, and play hostess. I suppose it's my way of surviving the assault to my heart. I hate it. It's not what I want to be doing but it's all my heart and body can do.

I don't sleep. I can't sleep. The thought of our bedroom makes me nauseous. I stay far away from Chris's and my room. I don't even shower in there.

———

January 13, 2015

Incredibly, Kelly has been able to get Savannah and Chris's brothers on the flight into Cuba today. I feel grateful (and impatient) to have the chance to put my arms around my oldest daughter.

Savannah flies home on January 13th. When my eyes land on her, my comfort level rises a notch. Over the next week, the three of us—my girls and me—build a cocoon of sorts around ourselves. This wall of protection and comfort, support and intimacy, will last forever. I can feel it. We feed off each other's strength and mourn with each other in the low moments. As alone as I feel, I also know I will never be truly alone. Not with my girls. Not with the bond we are building. I trust them implicitly, and they trust me. It's a weird change. I watch as Madison and Savannah grow immeasurably more mature in just a few days. They are quite amazing.

At times, in the near and long-range future, I will have to reign them in, but their loyalty and love sustain me, and my love fuels them. People talk about mama bears. But people should also take note of the fierce cubs she raises.

I introduce Mike and Hank to Kelly and others.

Arrangements, mourning, and NCIS activity are still spinning like a tornado in our little world. Much of the time, I just want to be alone. I run off to the bathroom simply to compose myself, take some breaths, or sit in silence. I am still overwhelmed and in shock.

There are conversations I want to have in private, but it's not long before Chris's brothers take exception to that. They think they should be a part of every discussion, every decision, and every piece of information. I disagree. This is the first time they have ever been to GTMO. Yes, Chris was their brother, but he was my husband. These are my friends. This is my home. Briefly, I think, "Am I offending them, too?

"No, I'm communicating my needs."

Yet they continue to push back, and they express frustration when I have discussions with others without their input. As an olive branch, I play tour guide and show them around the base, introducing them to people. I don't have the energy for this, but it's something they requested, so I try to oblige. I imagine they just want to feel close to the place where their brother spent the last four years.

I get the sense they also take exception when J.R. calls to check in with the family. He is the commanding officer on the base. I look at it as his duty to check in after a death like this, particularly since that's what friends do. Mike and Hank can't possibly understand the culture of GTMO. J.R. had done the same for others in the past—for any significant impact on a family. I don't find it unusual in the least.

I am struggling with the weight of everything happening. On top of grief and family dynamics, every time I turn around, like a mosquito on a summer evening, NCIS seems to be there. They interview me multiple times, and most of the time, I can't remember their questions or even my answers. My brain is still foggy. It's not just me. They are interviewing everyone. I can feel the slow burn of frustration and confusion. *Why are they in everyone's face right now?* I just don't get it, and my lack of understanding fuels the sizzle I feel in my chest. I think the timing of their presence and their questions are inappropriate, particularly when there are teenagers mourning the loss of their father. It feels like they are interrupting my ability to support my girls. Soon, I would learn why NCIS is everywhere and at all times.

I hear rumors. Patrice and Walter with NCIS seem to be in the middle of them, and rationally, I know they're doing their job. But I just want everything to stop. My girls and I cling to each other day and night. As their questions persist, they become more inappropriate, and I ask for Patrice to be removed from the case. She's grasping onto all of the rumors spreading on base, rumors about Captain Nettleton and me carrying on in a torrid love affair, that Chris caught us in bed together, that we were part of an underground sex ring. It's crazy! And she keeps asking why I put up with the abuse, why I didn't leave if it was so bad. I had been living with Chris's violent and controlling antics for two decades, and her lack of professionalism and repeated questions seem to point the finger in my direction. As if his abuse was my fault.

On several occasions, I ask to view Chris's body. I think seeing him will bring some measure of closure for me, emotionally and mentally. I am denied every time. J.R. first says I don't want to remember Chris this way. He explains how sea water causes people to bloat after death.

"It changes people, Lara. It's not how you will want to remember him," he tells me.

Others at NCIS give me a similar push back: "He won't look like the man you knew," they say. I relent, but no one is sharing any information with me. I feel shut out and closed off, which is making my grief harder to manage. I look at my girls, and I have no answers for them.

The next several days . . .

The days blend together. I can't get the *why* of Chris's death out of my head. I know Chris had drunk a lot that night. In one passing phone call, J.R. gives me an update:

"I feel we can preliminarily rule out suicide," he tells me.

J.R. reveals Chris had been fully clothed. He had his keys and phone in his pockets. His wedding band was in place, and his shoes were still on. We both know that in some cases, people who take their own lives have a plan and some, if not all, of these things are removed, set aside—even folded neatly. There were no indications Chris had planned anything. There is no note and no other physical signature for suicide.

I breathe in a gulp of air and slowly let it out. An ounce of relief envelopes me. I share with the girls and Chris's brothers that no one feels Chris took his life. And I find myself grateful with the news as I say it out loud. I hadn't known what to believe over these last few days, fully aware Chris had threatened such things in the past to get his way.

In the years that follow, Chris's family will communicate to others that I was telling people I believed Chris had taken his life. It's simply not true. I feared it. But I didn't know anything, and in those first few days, I couldn't even venture a guess as to what had happened that night once Kelly peeled an irate Chris off of me in the bathroom. My main concern was for my girls, and once J.R. said there were no indications Chris committed suicide, I believed him. The Tur Family's lies in this regard have been damaging to my girls, my reputation, and me.

Aside from the horror, grief, and loss that comes specifically with suicide, I know Chris would never have done that to our girls. And certainly, I didn't want to have to tell our girls that is how Chris left this world—that he didn't want to be with them anymore or that his love for them was outweighed by either his drunken decisions, his rage toward me, or his inability to live without me as his wife. That would have been the worst news I could have shared with Savannah and Madison. No way. I know Chris wouldn't leave them to spite me.

Chris had not been equipped to be a good husband. And he wasn't capable of always being a great dad, but he loved his girls. He loved me, too, in the only way he could, which unfortunately was through control and violence. He may have said nasty things about the girls to me to strong-arm me into doing what he wanted, but I knew he didn't mean what he said when he used the girls as weapons to overpower me in our marital games and disputes. I knew that.

I finally talk with the Navy Exchange. They inform me that Chris cancelled his life insurance years ago. I feel a bit dizzy. I still have my life insurance, insurance he had ensured was as adequate as his, but somehow, he had cancelled his? *Why would he do that?* The irony and betrayal cuts me to the core.

Even though the days become meshed together, I know we're inching closer to Saturday, the day of his services. Numerous people and departments pitch in to serve us in any way they can. MWR—Moral, Welfare, and Recreation—donates the food for the re-pass. I am grateful for every act of kindness.

Dawnell and Jose, Kelly's boyfriend, fly in from New York. Mark stays back but sends a letter to be read at the funeral, the eulogy to be read by another, mutual friend.

Saturday arrives, and the base is mostly closed. Nearly five hundred people make their way to the chapel. Some of the Marines arrive in full military dress. Even though we have no casket or ashes—Chris's body hasn't been released yet and is being prepared for transport to Pennsylvania for a family funeral—the Marines will be doing an honors ceremony since Chris was a former Marine. After Mark's eulogy is read, many others stand up to speak, mostly sharing how Chris was such an entertaining storyteller, a great dad and husband, and a true friend.

I know some of the stories people share are not true. I know some people have believed everything Chris ever said, even though I know, emphatically, he often lied or exaggerated, as these stories prove. But the ceremony is lovely, and I let it all go. I have to. I cannot carry that burden any longer.

With a shaky voice, Savannah gets up and speaks, and my heart feels the weight of her sorrow. She reads the last letter she had received from Chris, and it stirs tears in many of the mourners, myself included. It's the same letter she had raced away from Amy to retrieve the day I told her Chris was gone.

Now, it's time for the flag-folding, honor ceremony. I have been to one such ceremony—ten years ago. Chris's dad, an Air Force vet, was given a full honors guard at his funeral, complete with the flag-folding component. I look around and something feels off. For the first time, I notice some of the Marines are not in their full dress uniform. I assume things must be different since there is no casket and no ashes to include in the process. I don't think about it for too long as I get wrapped up in the movements of the ceremony. The First Sergeant of the Marine Corps leads the service at this point, and a servicemember presents me with a plaque and a small flag.

"Thank you for your service and sacrifice for our country, ma'am," he says, leaning down to hand me the items.

"Thank you," I say softly. I experience a moment. My intuition tells me something is wrong—a gut sense, if you will. I stare at the miniature flag and wonder why no one folded it as I had witnessed at Chris's dad's funeral. I look at the plaque, and there is a picture of the American flag, the one flying on base over the Northeast Gate at GTMO. I lay it on my lap. Tears spring forth, a cleansing cry, full of multiple emotions. Relief. Sorrow. And peace for both Chris and myself.

After the service, as people file out, and we plan to attend the barbeque dinner with close friends and family at the house, I thank the sergeant and ask him about the honors ceremony.

"Today's not the day to talk about it," he tells me.

I nod and follow the girls out, arm-in-arm.

That evening, back at the house, we grill burgers, and I sag into a chair, eyelids heavy, and watch as everybody gets drunk. I listen to them reminisce about Chris, re-telling the stories he told them. I listen to them rave about a man, as if he had hung the moon. I know no one ever would, or should, put down a person at their funeral. It's poor taste, but I prefer the saying, "If you don't have anything nice to say . . ." I sit quietly, not knowing this would be the last time I'd ever sit with some of these people in a social setting and call them friends.

CHAPTER 18

LIES AND BETRAYAL

"It is a proud privilege to be a soldier—a good soldier [with] discipline, self-respect, pride in his unit and his country, a high sense of duty and obligation to comrades and to his superiors, and a self-confidence born of demonstrated ability."
—George S. Patton, Jr.

It's Sunday. Chris's brothers, the girls, and I are scheduled to fly out tomorrow, Monday, with Chris's body to make the journey to Pennsylvania. The First Sergeant of the Marine Corps calls me. We live in the same neighborhood—he's actually right across the street.

This past week, I had given him power of attorney to collect Chris's military records so we could recreate his Marine uniform to display at the repass ceremony. The First Sergeant had spent the week collecting

153

Chris's documents, and I had collected the medals I knew were in our house. As a somewhat funny aside, Chris had used some of his medals to hang sheets in our first apartment when Savannah was born to act as curtains. With the receipt of the official documents, his uniform could hold the appropriate bars and insignias. I don't know the first thing about rank, bars, and other honors, so I had asked him for help with this.

At the repass, I noticed some of the honors on Chris's uniform. I didn't know what they all meant. So when the First Sergeant calls, I answer the phone, about to get one of the biggest surprises of my life.

"Lara, I'm sorry to have to tell you this, but Chris was not honorably discharged from the military," he tells me.

"What?" I squeeze the phone in an effort not to drop it. My mind spins.

"His discharge is listed as OTH," he explains. I know what the acronym stands for—other than honorably discharged. "He was discharged because of drugs, and he had three NJPs." I know this acronym, too. *Non-judicial punishments.*

"What?" It's all I can say.

Then I remember . . . "Wait, that's not possible. When I was pregnant, my doctor sent a Red Cross message to Chris in Okinawa so he could come home. I was having problems with my pregnancy. There was a Red Cross message—"

"I'm sorry, Lara. He was already in the middle of administrative review when he arrived in Okinawa. He had been in trouble before he got there." *That's why I couldn't be put on his orders after we were married.* My thoughts become rapid-fire at this point, connecting dots I had never been able to connect before.

This is why he would never check "VA benefits" for our mortgage applications.

This is why he would never go to the VA for healthcare.

When he had been home for Savannah's birth, he had received his dishonorable discharge. He had been kicked out of the military twenty years ago. The only paperwork I ever saw was what I now know is called a redacted DD214. It simply said he was no longer in the military. I would later learn there is an unredacted DD214 that explains Chris's OTH discharge due to drug abuse.

This is why Chris hadn't received a full-honors ceremony yesterday. What they did perform was modified and only out of respect for the girls and me. I believe it was likely out of respect for Chris, as well; he had been supporting the Marines in GTMO for a while now. But by all rights, even what they did should never have happened.

"You didn't know." I hear it as a statement, not a question. The First Sergeant is trying to be kind, and later, I would recognize that and feel grateful. Right now, I only feel blindsided, betrayed to a level I have never known.

"I didn't know," I repeat, softly. I figure out how to thank him and then punch off the call.

Was everything in our lives a lie?

My lips pinch together, and I can feel my furious heartbeat in my eardrums. Grief morphs into spitting anger in an instant. Nearly every outlandish story he had told about Okinawa was a lie. They were concoctions of others' stories, and I grew sick with the thought of how he had stolen true servicemembers' stories as his own. The magnitude of the lie envelopes me.

Semper Fidelis [Always Faithful]

Integrity

Honor

Chris's brothers walk into the room.

"What's wrong?" Mike asks.

I explain the news, spilling it out in frustration, looking for some outlet for my swirling emotions. Putting on the clothes of anger keeps me from the nakedness of pain. I tell them why the flag-folding honors ceremony was different than the one for their dad.

"We already know that," they respond. Quite matter-of-factly.

It's as if they have slapped me in the face. "What . . . how? I didn't know!" I feel confused, agitated.

They explain Chris had told them twenty years ago when he had returned from Japan. "He said he just wanted to be with you, so he did everything he could to get out of the military." *That's absurd.*

With the information the First Sergeant had shared and the timing of everything, I know that is a lie, too. He had already been under review when we were married. He had already experienced an NJP. I feel irritated with his brothers, but I dismiss it. I know it wasn't their responsibility to tell me. It was Chris's.

"We assumed you knew," they say. Their casual attitude rips me apart. I cannot believe they don't care that I didn't know.

"Nope," I reply. It's the only word I can muster.

This is a turning point. First, the cancelled life insurance policy. Now, I discover this lie that leaves us without benefits. I realize I'm dealing with a lot of stuff that most widows don't have to deal with—lies, betrayal, and fury. I feel myself shut down. It's almost instantaneous. I can no longer cope. I can't be okay for one more minute. This is all too traumatic for anyone to manage.

———

Tomorrow arrives, and is now called today. Mike and Hank are adamant about seeing Chris's body before we leave the island. They want to be able to assure their mom that Chris's body is, in fact, in the wooden box, his temporary casket for transport. The Coast Guard grants Mike and Hank access inside the Naval hospital to watch as they prepare the body and seal up the box.

When they see me afterward, they don't share anything with me. However, Mike persuades me to let him and Pam, his wife, make arrangements for a private autopsy to be performed in Pennsylvania. I don't have the energy to ask questions or even discuss it. I don't have the will to argue.

We head over to the airfield. The C-130 is a large transport plane used by the military, including for activities such as servicemembers jumping out of the back. It's a wide vessel with seating on the periphery and straps to hold you in place on the hard seat.

The girls and I board alongside Chris's brothers. Chris's body, inside the box, is placed in the center of the plane. We stare at it as we take off for the multi-hour trip to Norfolk, Virginia, the first leg of our journey. The girls grow uncomfortable. Each grabs a blanket and retires to a spot on the floor of the plane to rest.

We spend the night in Norfolk at the Little Creek Naval base while the transport continues on to Philadelphia with Chris's body. The next morning, we make our way to Chris's family's house in Montgomery County, Pennsylvania.

CHAPTER 19
THE ANONYMOUS "TIP"

"Gentle reader, may you never feel what I then felt! May your eyes never shed such stormy, scalding, heart-wrung tears as poured from mine. May you never appeal to Heaven in prayers so hopeless and so agised as in that hour left my lips: for never may you, like me, dread to be the instrument of evil to what you wholly love."
—Charlotte Brontë in *Jane Eyre*

January 20–22, 2015

Chris's family and my family converge in Montgomery and Bucks Counties in Pennsylvania. My parents stay with Ann, Chris's mom, as they had earlier, upon first hearing the news of Chris's death. They didn't want her to be alone. Now, they return so we can all be close to one another for the family's funeral services and burial.

Since Savannah's university campus is so close, Savannah stays in her dorm with her roommate, a close friend. Madison and I stay with Mike Tur's family in their home. That first day, we get settled and start to finalize the plans for the upcoming services and events.

By this time, I am dragging. We have already held services in GTMO, I have uncovered multiple lies Chris had never shared with me, and despite anxiety about how to pay for Savannah's college, I am trying to keep it together for my girls.

The next day, Chris's family talks about the independent autopsy and dates. Madison's birthday is coming up. She'll be fifteen on January 25th. I don't want anything to ruin her birthday, so I make a firm request that nothing related to Chris's funeral happens on her birthday weekend. Madi is alive, and I want to celebrate her.

"I know Chris will be cremated, but we cannot do anything on Madi's birthday. No interment, no funeral, no discussion of Chris, his death, or arrangements on the 25th. Everything stops for her birthday," I implore. Nobody disagreed.

We sit in Mike's family room. As we talk about locations for the various services, I feel some comfort in the familiarity of the area. The church where the funeral will be held is the same church where I used to work, where Madi went to preschool, and the girls and I attended church services all those years ago.

I look down at my hands. My fingers have turned into spindly protrusions, unrecognizable after losing so much weight these past couple of weeks and now getting used to the winter cold in the northeast. My body only knows tropical weather, and I rub my hands together for warmth. My four rings—a double wedding band, an anniversary band, and my engagement ring—slide off my ring finger. Afraid of losing them—there are close to three carats of diamonds set in these rings—I move them to my left pointer finger.

My shoulders sag. The room is tinged with chaos, a byproduct of Chris's large family. I am briefly reminded of how loud they can be as I think back to the early years when I first dated Chris. I feel no need to control all these moving parts, so when others ask to plan certain details themselves, I nod. Someone suggests having the repass—after-service dinner—at a restaurant called Braveheart to honor Chris's love of the movie with the same name. As long as we all reach the same destination, I don't care how we get there. I nod again. We discuss Chris's remains and the adjacent cemetery where his ashes can be interned. Then we talk about if that is even what we want to do . . . do we want to split them? Should I take them since I don't live in the States?

Ann suggests we save the ashes in necklaces, vials we can wear or store as some sort of jewelry-like keepsakes. Madison and Savannah have an immediate reaction.

"No way," they almost say in unison.

"That's creepy. We are not doing that," Savannah finishes. I couldn't agree more.

"No one is going to wear Chris's ashes around their neck," I add.

I am sitting next to my parents, and I look at them. I wonder if they think Chris's family is as obnoxious as I do. I can hear Mike talking to Aline about GTMO. I strain to hear what he's saying. I wonder why she is even interested. I appreciate her condolences, but Chris hasn't spoken her name for the last ten years. The girls don't know her, nor does she know them. She is not a part of our lives and hasn't been by Chris's design. She is his sister, but they had been estranged for more than a decade.

Out of the blue, Mike announces, "I think he was murdered." The air is sucked out of the room. Everyone freezes.

"Oh, for (explicative) sake. Are you kidding me?" I think my words were uttered under my breath, but I realize others have heard me. *What a looney toon!* I stand up and head outside for a cigarette. I can't take it anymore. The conspiracy theories. The fact that Mike and Hank were in GTMO for one week and return believing they have pieced together a mystery, the whole story—that they know everyone and everything. *What possible conversation could you have had that would lead you to believe that!* I am done with the soap boxes. I am done with Mike's pontification. I am done with this overbearing, chaotic, and paranoid family.

I slam the door on my way out. In the cold air, I inhale the nicotine, hoping it'll calm my nerves and irritation, and then hold my breath. I can hear Aline adding her two cents, as if she knows anything about her brother at all. She is the last person who should be speaking right now.

After a few minutes of solitude, I reenter Mike's house. I have no idea what else has transpired while I've been outside, but they have stopped talking about it.

Once my body feels the heat of the house again, I question the sanity of it all:

Why can't his family be normal?
Why can't we just be a normal group of grieving people?
Why is his family so dysfunctional?

Later that evening, the house is busy with people. I relax with a small group in what had been Mike and Pam's dining room. They live in a Colonial-style, traditional house. No open floor plan. I can hear cousins in the basement and others in the kitchen talking. Some are in the family room watching TV.

For Christmas, they had converted their dining room to a sitting room for a large get-together they had hosted. There are comfy chairs around the periphery and a coffee table in the middle. A window on one of the pale-yellow walls overlooks the backyard. Mike sits to my right, and Savannah is across from me. He is trying to teach us the game of spoons. I am really not interested, and after a while, some of the girls—Savannah and her friend included—grab their phones and begin to scroll. I'm in my own little world of thoughts and fatigue, still feeling irritated about Mike's earlier supposition.

I know I'm just going through the motions with family, but I can't help it. I'm coasting. When someone asks me something, I simply nod or shake my head. I'm not really up for many words at this point. It's as if I can see everybody, including myself, from outside the group, as if I'm floating above it all. An outsider, but still part of the nightmare.

My phone rings and cuts through my hazy existence. I pull it out of my pocket and see it's Dawnell calling.

"Hey," I say.

Without preamble, she says, "You're on TV."

"What?" I try to release the fogginess from my brain.

"Lara, you're all over the news. You're everywhere. It's everywhere."

"What are you talking about?" I ask.

As Dawnell's voice sounds in my ear, I see Savannah look up from her phone. In her maturity, she doesn't freak out but stays calm. Without a word, she turns her phone so I can see the screen. There it is. A headline article.

Captain Nettleton has been relieved of his position at GTMO
Suspicious death of Christopher Tur
Alleged affair
Possible murder . . .

I was already numb, but now I feel myself being sucked into a black hole. The chaos of the house becomes silence. Momentarily, I think I've lost my hearing.

Just as suddenly as the noise disappeared, the house erupts in chaos. My ears are pierced with the transition from my mute environment to the loudest ruckus I've ever heard. As discreet as Savannah was when she had turned the phone to me, it seems every person in the house now knows about the article.

"What?"

"Oh my gosh!"

"I can't believe this!"

People are yelling from the family room where they watch the TV. Others are screaming as the news breaks on their phones. The people in the dining-room-turned-sitting room look at me, their faces expressing their confusion, questions, and yes, anger.

"I don't know . . . I don't know." It's all I can say.

And then everything turns to black.

———————

The next thing I remember is light. It's day time, January 22, and I don't remember ever going to bed. I don't remember waking up in a bed. I am just suddenly aware I'm standing in Mike's kitchen. I have no idea how I got here. I can't remember the rest of last evening, who was there, who had left before the news . . . yes, I remember the news. I wonder who I spoke with, if anyone, and I wonder what I said to them. I just don't know. My memory has been torn into fragmented pieces. (I have spent years trying to recollect the rest of that evening, and I have not been able to do so.)

There are a few others in the kitchen with me, including Madison. There are news vans and media on the street. I have no idea how they found me. *And so quickly.* Found all of us. Rapid calls have been coming in to all family members, on both sides. Most don't answer or reply with, "No comment." Everyone seems to be milling around the house or watching the news on TV. I hear phones still ringing in every corner of the house.

Madison looks up from her phone. "Mom, Julia wants to know if it's okay if Mr. Nettleton calls you?" My sweet Madi. In the future, we would talk about this moment often. Madison is friends with J.R.'s daughter. All the kids on base are friends. It's just that kind of close-knit community. And she's called J.R. "Mr. Nettleton" for as long as I can remember. He never minds; he knows she's a kid—not even fifteen yet—and in her world, he's simply her friend's dad.

It still pains me deeply that our children, my children, were thrown into the middle of this. The deep judgment they experience, how they become vile pawns, all of it will start today and continue for years to come. This has caused me to experience more anger than anything else.

The chatter in the kitchen and family room stops. I feel everyone's eyes bore into me.

"Sure," I say.

I walk outside for privacy, and Mike follows me. I cannot believe it. My gut turns at this intrusion and reminds me of the many times Chris used to interrupt my conversations with others or stalk me while I was on the phone with friends, asking me what we were talking about.

"What are you doing?" I ask him.

"I came out here for your phone call," he responds, matter-of-factly, as if I need a babysitter.

"I'm fine," I reply firmly. Now it feels awkward. As politely as I can, I say, "This is none of your business." I hadn't asked J.R. to call me, and I don't have any idea what he is going to say to me. But I know I don't need a chaperone for whatever it is. Even if this were my parents following me out the door, I would have asked them to leave, too. I think, *I don't even do this to my teenage girls with their phone calls.* It is not a personal affront to Mike; it's simply a private conversation.

Mike turns around and goes back inside. I am grateful, though it's obvious he's irritated by the way he enters his house—closing the door forcibly behind him with a dirty look thrown my way. I sigh and wait for my phone to ring.

J.R. calls a minute or two later.

"Hi, how are you doing?" he asks. I am still in the "I'm fine. I'm good" mentality with few words to spare, and that's the answer I give him. There is really nothing else to say. I mean, my picture is all over the Internet. I am walking through the second set of funeral services for Chris, the man who had spent our whole marriage lying to me and making me feel like a caged animal, and now this. There are no words to express how I am doing.

"Well, I want to tell you some things that I want you to hear from me and not through the news or from others."

"Okay," I say without emotion. I know I can't take any more, so I suppose my body is blocking me from feeling anything more.

J.R. tells me about a fight he and Chris had the night Chris went missing, a fight after everyone left The Bayview and the Officers' Club. He tells me how Chris showed up at his house, entered without being let in, and punched J.R. in the back of the head. J.R. goes into detail about that night: how Chris was bouncing around emotionally, how they scuffled and threw punches, fighting each other after Chris initially sucker-punched him, how his daughter was home and Chris knew that, how Chris let him go console Julia, and how when J.R. returned, Chris was gone.

"Lara, he was so unstable. He'd call me names and yell at me, saying he hated me and asking why I was sleeping with his wife, and in the next second, he was asking if I wanted to go have a drink at the bar. He went from being in a rage to being broken, saying he didn't want to lose you."

J.R. explained they'd fight and then talk and then Chris would rage again, so they fought again.

I stand outside Mike's house, incredulous, listening to J.R.'s account of that part of the night, a part I had known nothing about. I can't believe Chris had the audacity to blow into the CO's home and assault him. The XO had sent him home from the Hail and Farewell. *Why was Chris so stupid? Why didn't he just go home that night?*

"Thank you for telling me," I say when J.R. finishes. I can't find any other words. My anger returns. In the privacy of my own mind, I yell at Chris, though he's no longer here:

You are crazy! You left your family high and dry—a dishonorable discharge that came like a thief. But you made sure, up until the moment you died, that everyone considered you a hero. Even though you treated me like s***. You leave me with your cuckoo family. And now this! What else will I have to clean up? What else do I need to know, Chris?

As we get ready to hang up the phone, J.R. tells me he'll check in and keep in contact. "I'll be fine," I reply. I'm not even sure what that means, but I'm grateful for his kindness. I realize I now have to re-enter Mike's house. I have to face everyone. And now that I've spoken with J.R., I don't know what to expect from them. I just know I feel so alone.

———

Inside, the air is warm but the company is not. I feverishly think about what I am supposed to say to Chris's family. They are all here: Ann, Mike and Pam, Hank and Sandy, Aline and her husband. Savannah has left to stay with a friend. She needed to get away. My parents are keeping Madison busy and distracted, and I am grateful.

It's been two weeks since Chris's death, and I am just now privy to a fight that happened on the base that night. My thoughts swirl in bits and pieces. I can't make sense of anything.

Later, I won't be able to remember much of these two days, not every movement nor what was said to me but only my thoughts. It will take me years and help from my daughters to put some of these fractured memories and moments back together.

I move toward the kitchen. My mind can't stop:

Chris hasn't even been buried yet.

My face and name are all over the global news.

The Today Show*!*

Chris lied about his honorable discharge.

He assaulted J.R. before he went missing!

I know I have to talk to Madison and Savannah. We had agreed no secrets during this time. They aren't children anymore. Savannah is eighteen, and in a couple days, Madison will be fifteen. They don't want to be protected, but at the same time, I have to protect them. This has become such a hot mess, such a twisted and chaotic time in our lives. I feel for them, but if I feel too much, I know I'll shut down again.

I become a walking body. No emotions. No more thoughts. No decisions. I just can't do it. I feel no more anger, nor sadness, nor cares. Everything turns to auto-pilot as I try to prevent myself from falling into oblivion and not being able to support my children.

My parents can tell I've totally shut down, and they step in to help. They are concerned about safety for my girls and me, and that's when I retain my first attorney. I know I have to get some of my faculties together to speak to a lawyer. My parents want to be sure that, legally, we are protected through this media coverage. I finally have someone else to speak out about some of the things I am thinking: This is wrong to leak this kind of inflammatory information without evidence and without our knowing. My kids need to be protected. How can the news go so public with these "allegations," a term they are using, when there are children involved?

After I speak with the attorney, I feel a bit relieved. They will do the legal legwork now, and I can focus on my daughters and me.

It's still late morning. I sit at the kitchen table and try to eat, but I am numb. Suddenly, Mike is towering over me.

"I think it would be best if you and Madison found somewhere else to stay," he says.

"Okay," I say. There is no argument. Part of me has become agreeable to anything, just to make this whole situation stop. "Okay" has become my go-to solution to avoid any more emotional turmoil. The other part of me doesn't feel safe here in this house anyway. His family hasn't been supportive, nor willing to see reality or hear the truth about Chris. And their need to be a part of my every movement, as if it's their right, is suffocating.

I collect Madi's and my bags, and my parents, knowing this was coming in some way, have already booked us a hotel room. While I'm packing, Mike has the audacity to ask me for a copy of Chris's "honors" service in GTMO.

"Okay," I say. Again, it is just easier. I give him a copy.

Just last night, before the news broke with these "allegations," Mike and Pam had asked me to quit my job at GTMO and offered Madison and I a place to live with them. Now this. I hadn't taken his request seriously. Why would I quit the job I love? Why do you think I can't take care of my daughters and myself? *I'm not a feeble woman.* Now, the 180-degree turn is both confusing and shows how unwilling Chris's family is to even listen to me. Madi and I haven't been here seventy-two hours before we aren't welcome anymore.

After we transfer to the hotel, I wake up on Friday to the front page of the *USA Today*. There we are, directly above Tom Brady's statement about not knowing there were deflated footballs. *Oh, my gosh!*

CHAPTER 20

MANIPULATED BY "FAMILY"

"The ultimate measure of a man is not where he stands in moments of comfort and convenience, but where he stands at times of challenge and controversy."
—Martin Luther King, Jr.

While at the hotel, my friend, Amy, and I keep the girls distracted and entertained, inviting them to go experience places rather than sit in a cramped hotel room all day and night.

We take photos of ourselves and the girls. In one, it's evident my rings aren't on my ring finger; they still rest safely on my pointer finger. The photo is posted to social media, and Chris's family has a field day, claiming disrespect and unfaithfulness on my part. I now live my life under an unrelenting and harsh microscope.

During this time, I also exchange emails and paperwork with his family. It's not pleasant. There is still a funeral service to be conducted. Even though we have been kicked out of their house, we still have to finalize arrangements.

Hank and Sandy come to the hotel and ask me to sign a document they printed from their computer. They tell me it would help out with the funeral logistics, saying they couldn't do anything at the funeral home without it. I believe them and sign the paper.

We had already discussed Chris's cremation and there are so many moving parts; as I said, if we all get to the same destination, I don't care how it's done or who fills what cog in the wheel. I actually appreciate the assistance. There is so much to handle when your spouse dies.

Saturday comes, and it's the day we all agreed we'd celebrate Madi's fifteenth birthday. Madison wants to go to a Japanese hibachi restaurant where they cook the food in front of you. Ever since we had moved to GTMO, she has missed those types of restaurants; they just don't have anything like them on base. I agree, and we all meet there. Amy and her boyfriend, Todd—whom I am meeting for the first time—my family, including my brother and his wife and children, and Chris's family are all together—even Aline and Pat, people Madison doesn't know at all. Inside, I feel disrupted. *They think they can just insert themselves into our lives at this point? That they have some sort of stake in our family?*

At the end of our meal and the opening of presents, I pay the bill—$1,300. While I am content to cover the costs of Madi's birthday celebration, I am left a bit worried about our future financial situation, and I feel somewhat surprised that no one, except my parents, offers to help pay for the large group meal. There are over a dozen of us there! I decline my parents' offer. I already feel like a failure. I don't think I should accept every offer of assistance from them; they're already hiding me in a hotel, listening to me cry into the wee hours of the morning, and keeping my girls busy. They are my foundation, and I don't want to do anything that will crack it.

Over the next week, Savannah and I are served subpoenas for Chris's ashes. Chris's family had taken them, unauthorized, from the funeral home. Over text messages, they tell me they are going to have a funeral with full honors. *That's why Mike wanted a copy of the service from GTMO.*

They plan to use photos from the CD that was created in GTMO, as if it was part of their own memories. His family also pulled quotes from our friends, and are twisting them into convenient lies to fit their narrative of who they want Chris to have been. They want a flag-folding ceremony. *They are literally stealing the Marine's playbook.* I lose it when I hear they plan to tell a story at the funeral that Chris enacted "global change" in the military system world-wide. As a loss prevention supervisor, he did no such thing. I certainly never saw any Congressional accolades for his "global initiatives."

You can't do that, I type back.

He was dishonorably discharged.

Chris's family doesn't care. They even go so far as to solicit Mark's help—as former commanding officer for the Marines in GTMO, and he politely declines. "I can't help you. He can't have full honors," he tells them.

On multiple fronts and by numerous people, Chris's family is told they can't proceed with their plans. They don't listen. They don't care. In fact, they are preparing to present several folded flags to people, something you don't even see in the movies.

I feel sick, ashamed that I have anything to do with this family. They are dishonoring the U.S. military. I talk to Savannah about it—remember, no secrets—and she explodes.

While in school, Savannah has been working with the MWR, Morale Welfare and Recreation department. In the future, it's where she will end up working. The Liberty Center, as it's called, is a group of young, unaccompanied, active members.

"No!" she yells when I explain the Tur family's plans. "He's not a fallen hero! It's offensive! They can't do that!" She is beside herself. "If they do that, I won't go. I'm not going to be a part of dishonoring our service members."

I cannot disagree. She asks me to reply to his family and tell them how inappropriate it is. I tell her I've already done that. And because of the letter Hank and Sandy had me sign a few days earlier, they have permission to pick up the ashes from the funeral home, and that's just what they do. My fury boils over. I send an email to the church to cancel the service, and the Turs text me to say they are going to hold the service whether I like it or not.

You no longer have a choice, their message reads.

Oh, that's nice, I think. I cannot believe we are here, in this space of immaturity and lies. That Hank and Sandy would have me sign a document under false pretenses, giving them power over Chris's ashes. It's despicable. This is a mockery to the Marines, and honestly, I don't want any part of it. Or them.

Both Madison and Savannah are angry with Chris's family, too. I don't think it can get any worse. I am wrong. I discover Chris's family filed legal documents stating Chris and I had been "physically separated" since October 2014. This is what gave them the right to take the ashes. *Who do they think they are? They haven't been a part of our lives in GTMO! They've never been there, except Mike and Hank for Chris's service three weeks ago! They saw that Chris and I were living in our house!*

Lies. More lies. I can't take it. How they could make this accusation is beyond me. The Tur family has just blatantly lied in court documents.

I feel their betrayal and outright dishonesty like punches to my face and stomach. I am living in disbelief that they would put Savannah and Madison through all this. Feeling helpless, I hire attorney number two to fight for Chris's ashes. He was my husband. For better or worse, he was the girls' dad. I feel an obligation to fight for his remains . . . for them. My cage shrinks as I pay for this attorney. And for the first time, I feel as if the girls have crawled inside the cage with me. It triggers a sadness I've never known.

The judge, with one foot out of the door toward a vacation, requests us all to settle.

"Don't make me miss my vacation," was his message. I'm now $11,000 deep into this battle, and in the end, I settle for a quarter of Chris's ashes. I find this all to be so ridiculous. The Tur family purchases a headstone, complete with a false narrative of who he was, and my children are offended by it. Lance Corporal U.S.M.C. Because of all the disciplinary actions against him, Chris was a Private First Class when he was kicked out of the military. This is not something he would ever have put on his headstone.

The Tur family writes me out of the obituary. It's as if I never existed. Another slap in the face, especially when I had included Aline in Chris's obituary at GTMO. I had left no one out to keep the peace and for the sake of my girls, not wanting history or anger to position my choices. They didn't do the same for me. They only want to create discord and hate in a public forum.

Some may ask, "Why does it matter?" For one, Chris had been my husband for nearly twenty years, and he was my children's father. I resign to the idea that the girls and I already had closure in Cuba. The service there was our good-bye to him. We honored him with the people who knew us best, our family at GTMO.

The edict from the settlement dictates that Savannah and Madison are the only ones allowed to touch the ashes. More ridiculousness. I can't even accept them on their behalf. So my dad drives Savannah and me to get our portion of Chris's remains from the funeral home. Even the funeral director is repulsed by this display, disgusted by what the Tur family is doing to my girls and me.

"I'm so sorry about all of this," he says to my dad and me.

As we're leaving, Mike and Pam approach us.

"We want to talk to Savannah," they say.

I look at Savannah and instantly know she has no interest in having a private conversation with them. She shakes her head, and they grab her. Savannah is trying to hold the ashes and get into my dad's car as she shakes herself loose.

In my marriage, I was submissive to Chris's physical affronts. When it comes to my kids, I will not tolerate it. As Mike puts his hands on my daughter, it sets off a fire in me. "Get your hands off my child," I yell. She's eighteen, but she will always be my child.

"You have no right . . . she doesn't want to talk to you," I continue.

"We can talk to her whenever we want to," Mike spits back. I can't believe what I'm hearing.

"No, you can't," I say.

Savannah looks terrified. My dad intervenes. "Back away from my car," he demands.

Finally, they move away, but my daughter is clearly shaken. She sits in the back and doesn't say a word. I say what I can to try to help, apologizing that she has been put in the middle of all this adult drama—drama that doesn't have to be.

I think, *My kids shouldn't have to deal with the brunt of this! Their faces shouldn't be in the news. People shouldn't be grabbing them!"*

Unbeknownst to me, as she sits in the backseat of my dad's car, Savannah texts Chris's family. In her messages, she is showing every bit of her independence. She is frenzied, and her texts, I would learn later, are very colorful and angry. In them, she tells Mike, in no uncertain terms, she never wants to see him again—not under any circumstances. She is a frightened eighteen-year-old, and in these moments, she thinks these texts are worth it.

In the days to come, I would be accused of sending them while impersonating her. That is rubbish. When that doesn't stick, his family would also later accuse me of brainwashing my children. Wrong again. Years of living in an abusive home and then being manipulated by your dad's family after his death—that is the root of Savannah's outrage. These text messages are Savannah's way of finding her own path and becoming the person she wants to be—outspoken, independent, and someone with solid boundaries.

The attacks on me about my children become the tip of the iceberg. The Tur family, over the coming months and years, will send emails and letters to various people in my life, past and present. They will create open communication with the Navy Exchange, to the point that Chris's former boss will side with them, forgetting how he used to get drunk at our house when he visited GTMO, and Savannah would drive him back to his hotel. In the end, The Navy Exchange would give Ann Chris's Global War on Terrorism medal, something we both received for working in GTMO, rather than offer it to Savannah and Madison.

A smear campaign ensues. Employers, my family members, my friends and contacts at GTMO, and even my high school graduating class will receive communication from Chris's family, outlining what a horrible person I am. If there is a microphone or a keyboard, they will do their darndest to throw me and my girls under the bus with their two cents on a story they know very little about. While painful and harmful to my girls and my reputation, in the end, these tactics only reveal the true character of each of the Tur family members.

CHAPTER 21

RED TAPE

"Integrity is surely not a conditional word. It sways not to the rhythm of the winds nor ever change with the weather. As integrity is the honest, innermost image of self that dictates character."
—Chris Njenga

The girls and I try to move on, but it's difficult. Savannah flees the public eye to heal from the trauma of her dad's death, the news media's abuse of her image, the NCIS investigators still hounding us all, and the Tur family's dishonest and dishonorable maneuvering. She bounces from location to location so no one can catch up to her, trying to find peace. She takes our portion of Chris's ashes with her, though her hosts don't know about them. Savannah didn't want them in her dorm room or where scrutiny of any kind might occur. Madison and I can't take them because I would have to "touch them," and while I know this is absurdity, I abide by the court order. I want to be respectful and model the integrity I pray my kids grow up to emulate. And at this point, I don't want the ashes anyway. There is too much chaos attached to them.

Madison and I move to a second hotel with my parents to avoid much of what Savannah is hiding from. Next, we move in with my parents for a short time in New York. All the while, I try to close out Chris's accounts as the executor of his estate and move into probate. I had no idea there are so many steps and logistics involved in the death of a spouse. It's January in the Northeast, and winter weather has closed the court houses, making progress slow.

Because our legal address is our last permanent address in the States, Madi and I have to travel to Virginia for probate. Flights are cancelled, but we finally make it there. Once in Virginia, I receive an email from the XO at GTMO. He warns me about the time I've taken away from my job. I am floored. If I were anybody else, I don't think I would be reading an email like this. When Chris had taken leave from the Navy Exchange—leave which he hadn't yet earned since he was new there at the time—for his dad's funeral ten years ago, no one blinked. People in GTMO frequently donate time to those going through hardship (or celebration) when they need time off. Friends and coworkers had donated time to me in the past when I had taken Savannah to the States for a medical procedure. But now, no one offers me any assistance. I try not to panic, but I feel abandoned.

I sit up at night and think. The only thing I did wrong was engage in a one-night indiscretion in a hotel room in Florida. There was no "affair," and I certainly didn't have anything to do with, nor have any knowledge about, Chris's death. The injustice of what's happening to my girls and me rocks me to my core. I feel the Scarlet letter from across the Bay and several states away. It burns into my chest. And I think it's unfair. People are soaking in the news reports as if they contain "the whole truth and nothing but the truth." I can't believe they are entertaining the Tur family's characterization of their son, even though most of them know about the violent rages, the threats against me, the holes in the walls, the drunken outbursts, and the lies he fed his friends. I sit up and think through countless nights, dumbfounded by what is happening.

The icing on the cake comes when I hear the woman who has been temporarily assigned to my job while I'm tending to Chris's funeral arrangements and settling his estate in the States has been telling people I'm being replaced, and she is taking my position permanently. I have been discussing my plans with my parents and others. Before the story broke all over the news, I had been offered sponsorship to stay in GTMO. I was hoping to return to my role as director of the Fleet and Family Support Center, but now . . . I am not sure. I feel lost. In limbo. And it hurts.

A few days later, fear erupts in my soul again, replacing the numbness. The majority of people in GTMO seem to have become turncoats against me. The lies in the media are fueling them and helping them to shape their own stories of the past four years. I'm not sure it's safe to return. Rumors continue to prevail, and ninety-nine percent of them are untrue, but I can't defend myself. Yes, I slept with the captain of the base. Once. In an emotionally twisted night of despair but also in a realization that a better life was available to me. One devoid of abuse. What we did was wrong, but oh goodness, readers, it was also so right—for me. That one time of adultery (yes, I will name it and own it) was the stepping stone I needed to build up my resolve, to find a path forged by self-care, self-protection, and self-love. To end my victimization. And now, I feel victimized again—by NCIS, by the media, by the Tur family, and by those who are buying every piece of the news' stories without knowing or being willing to hear the other side. Even people whom I consider friends. No one wants to talk about the domestic violence case. No one wants to admit the new XO ignored my pleas for help the night Chris went missing and apparently assaulted the CO and later died. No one wants to admit there is a backstory to this breaking global news story.

My GS12 position is in jeopardy. I'm told I have to move to a priority replacement list. I have only two options from which to choose. Both are demotions. I start the paperwork amidst my heartbreak and fear.

March 2015

We are in Jacksonville, Madi and I, to prepare for our return to GTMO. The day before our flight, I meet with the region regarding my job and the status. I think it's fairly late in the game to be discussing all this. As I sit in the offices, I share with them my concerns about safety and security, my job, my aspirations, and my future. The group of professionals, many of whom have degrees in counseling and/or experience helping service members and their families—the ones who have provided services such as domestic violence support and counseling, family counseling, and job placement support to thousands of people—simply sit and stare at me. They ask me: "What do you want us to do?"

It takes everything in me not to say, "Your jobs!" I feel fury that here is a woman (me) asking for help, the same type of help I have spent years organizing for others, and I'm hitting the same roadblock that has been in place for decades.

"I need your help," I say again. Nothing. I feel like I'm begging. I erupt into tears, no longer able to keep myself together. There's still nothing. No response.

Over future years, people will ask me, "Why didn't you ask for help sooner?" when they hear about the domestic abuse, the violence, and the financial handcuffs I experienced as Chris's spouse.

This. Is. The. Reason.

Where would I have gone for help? The help I now require, which is all too public, is still elusive. No one offers counseling. No one offers financial assistance. No one has offered support in the way of donated time or advocacy. Now, no one offers job placement support. No one in the government or the Navy is fighting for me.

This is the reason I never said anything before. Historically and now presently, the Navy and government have swept domestic violence under the rug. They ignore lies. They protect their own—in this case, the new XO at GTMO. To support me, to believe me, is to say he was in the wrong when he ignored my pleas for help and didn't follow up to ensure Chris went home that night.

I knew if I reported Chris, he would hurt me. At best, my sponsorship would end, and I'd lose my home and my job, my career, because of someone else's abuse toward me. Victims are punished in our current system.

I know there are countless others, spouses and children neck-deep in homes filled with abuse or neglect. I know I am not the only one who suffered in silence, fearing the ramifications of seeking out help. I know there are spouses, right now, held in metaphorical chains, unable to seek out help, and it causes me much distress. I had spent years at GTMO working toward ways to change policies and rewrite curriculum to get support for these women. And now, I need help, and it's isn't here. All I want is to return to my job safely, to the job where I can continue working toward change. I am told that's not possible.

Madi and I fly back to GTMO. The base has recruited another temporary director in the role I once held. She is phenomenal, older and experienced. We sit and talk. She is, without a doubt, caught in the middle of this storm, and I know she's doing everything she can. But she must play both sides. I'm grateful for a neutral party to at least listen.

She tells me I can still work, but in a meeting with the XO, he strips me of my keys.

"How am I supposed to get in the building to work without keys?"

"They'll let you in," he replies. *So I have to ask permission to work?* "We also need your phone."

"What? No way," I say. "I have a daughter on base, and we don't feel safe here. What if she needs me?" I argue. "I'm not giving up my phone."

The XO becomes hostile, his voice rising. I interrupt his excuses.

"Go (explicative) yourself," I say. I feel cut down, stripped of my dignity. I have never given anyone any reason to suspect me of wrongdoing. My work here had been impeccable. I am a woman of integrity (unlike my late husband). The injustice and hypocrisy overwhelms me. "I did not create the problem here!" I feel like an enemy at every turn. Stuck. And I can't just grab Madi and drive off. We're on an island in the Caribbean. I understand in this moment, my time here is limited. In part because I want it to be; I am afraid.

I convey this to others—family, friends, and attorneys—over and over. It doesn't seem they can understand.

———————

In the weeks that follow, the XO and the Chief of Staff become inappropriate in their handling of the situation . . . at least to the degree that I become aware of everything they say and do related to Chris's death. They talk about him in the office, for public consumption and where everyone can hear, even though much of the information is either confidential or exaggerated.

"He had so many drugs in his system, they would have killed him anyway." First, this implies suicide or foul play. People hearing this would assume there's a secret story—one that just doesn't exist. I had been given a full autopsy report, and my copy didn't say that. *Stop spreading those rumors! My daughter is on the base! What kind of leaders are you?*

They also talk about Chris's death in their homes, in front of their children, and then those children go to school, saying things to Madi. Things, again, children shouldn't be involved with or know about, things that are lies or half-truths, and this creates division in the high school. Kids are forced to pick sides, and some stand up for Madi, trying to protect her.

I am beside myself with how the base and the XO are handling this.

"Peanut, I don't think it's true. I haven't heard that," I tell her. "They're just jerks," I conclude. I wish they'd stop putting kids in the middle of all this. All because some anonymous source leaked this garbage to the media on January 21, a source that didn't want to be named. I know it's crass, but I keep thinking, *My vagina has nothing to do with Chris's death! I am a civilian, not a military servicemember. What I did one night in October—what I do today—is my choice. There was no murder! No suicide!*

———

My husband was not a nice person. As I pack up our home in GTMO, I find more documents and records, which he had stashed— more proof I didn't know this man at all. During the course of our marriage, I knew about one DUI. I found the records of others, issued from multiple states, including North Carolina. His license had been suspended a couple of times. And there are so many tickets. At one point, the courts had recommended alcohol counseling. I knew none of this until now.

I also learn Chris was terminated from a job earlier in our marriage because he didn't show up for an entire week. I find job applications where he lied about his experience and accolades. I see how he applied multiple times for VA benefits and to reverse his OTH discharge status, and each one had been denied.

In the pit of my stomach, I feel the embarrassment and shame—not of his lies or indiscretions, but of not knowing. That I had somehow chosen poorly when I married this person and entrusted him with everything. Shame that most of my life has been built on untruths and secrecy. I feel responsible, in some twisted way, and at times apologize for his choices and behavior. On some level, I know I am carrying his burdens with that shame, but I can't help it.

With each passing day, as I continue collecting medical records, I discover more. He had been diagnosed with depression. He never told me. He was frequenting the base hospital to get medications, including Prozac and Atarax, medications one shouldn't take with alcohol. I didn't know this either. In the paperwork, he had checked that he wasn't a drinker. *Who was this person?*

With slow realization, I think, *Chris never told the truth. He was a compulsive, habitual liar.* My head spins. How does someone get away with so many secrets for so long?

―――――――

As I'm wading through all this, the government offers me three options for relocation. All are demotions to term—temporary—GS9 positions: Corpus Christi, Pensacola, or Jacksonville.

They promise me they'll max out my salary, but there will be no room for promotions any time soon.

"Don't worry," they say. "We'll find you a permanent position later."

It feels like a pat on the head and a shove in the back. I had worked hard to reach the role of department head. I wither under the weight of being dismissed. I can't believe they think I should feel grateful.

Even though Madi and I know people in Jacksonville, and that open position is the most appealing, J.R. and his family had been moved to

Jacksonville after he was let go as CO from GTMO. I know I can't go there. I can see the headlines now . . .

Jacksonville? Are they serious?

I cross off that option immediately. I don't need more drama in my life. Neither do my girls. I cannot go to Corpus Christi, either. For reasons not meant for this book, I want to avoid more drama there, as well. I don't want to follow someone else who had left GTMO for Corpus Christi under difficult circumstances. I don't want to make Corpus Christi the place where all the rejected people go. That leaves Pensacola. I know nothing about the base there, so I text friends who might. Each replies:

It's nice. You'll like it.

It's beachy and beautiful.

So the decision is effectively made for me. Pensacola it is.

Madison and I put all our belongings on the barge, the only way to move off the island. Then we pack our allotted luggage and carry-ons for the plane. Except our bags and suitcases are filled with atypical items. Rather than clothes and personal items, we pack all the things we cannot lose. I stuff my bags with paperwork, all the medical records, documents, and emails I know I can't lose. I just don't trust anyone right now. To Madi, I advise:

"Pack things that cannot be replaced. Forget clothes and shoes. We can buy more of those. Pack your photo albums, pictures, diary, and anything else you don't want to lose." My implication is "or have taken."

Madi and our big, potato of a dog—a pit mix weighing eighty pounds—and I board the plane out of GTMO. There is no send-off like most people receive. Ours will be memorable, but filled with sadness and loneliness.

When we arrive in Pensacola, the base informs me there is no more housing, something they never mentioned before. At this point, the government stops paying for our transition. Our orders and sponsorship, still a part of Chris, cover transport off the island only. Now I am on my own dime. Zero assistance.

We find a hotel close to base, and it's disgusting, but after having to rent a car and now pay for a hotel, it's all we can afford. Our two cars and our belongings won't arrive on the barge for quite some time.

I am required to start my job in one week. I have five days to get Madi enrolled in school, figure out housing, and get settled as a single mom. Madi and I feel alone, though my mom comes down for support.

On April 1, 2015, I start my new job as a work and family life specialist. The date will prove to be poetic.

CHAPTER 22
MY GLASS CEILING

"Throughout history, it has been the inaction of those who could have acted; the indifference of those who should have known better; the silence of the voice of justice when it mattered most; that has made it possible for evil to triumph."
—Haile Selassie

On April Fool's Day, I walk into a job where everybody already knows me, but I know no one. Well, they don't really *know* me. They know what they've seen and read in the news. I feel awkward—on display. I don't imagine any of the forty people in this building haven't seen *The Today Show*, "NBC Nightly News," or read the *Navy Times*. And they act like it. I feel the stares, smell their curiosity, and hear the quiet chatter throughout the day.

What makes it worse is that in my welcome conversation with the department head, she tells me the CO of the base doesn't want me there, but not to worry, she had fought for me. She believes this information is encouraging to me in some way, as if she's building rapport between her and I. But it does the opposite. *The CO doesn't even want me here.*

I understand his opinion, I carry the burden of headlining media stories, but on the other hand, I have done nothing wrong. My work record is flawless and filled with praise. I have given no one any reason to doubt my ability to do a great job, and as far as character . . . well, the news exaggerates. They want people to read their stories.

The only thing I am focusing on now is my job. I want to rebuild my life and move on. It seems no one will let me. So many have already made up their minds about me. There is one exception, a blessing, and she is my new officemate.

Rachel is kind, and we develop a close relationship. In the coming months, her compassionate nature propels me forward, and she turns into a great friend. Friends have become few and far between at this point, so gratitude solidifies our relationship. This closeness gives me hope during a dark season.

I begin counseling. I pay for it privately, no support comes from the government, with whom I still work. I know I am completely wrecked and need help to navigate what has happened to me. I am not sleeping. Every time I close my eyes, I relive the entire month of January, especially the night Chris went missing. I relive the last moment we had together when he tackled me on the sofa in the restroom. I relive the horrors of the past six months, and I just can't make the flashbacks stop, so I avoid sleep. There are times I go for days without resting, and then my body simply shuts down, and I pass out. I know I can't keep living like this. So in addition to counseling, I visit a doctor for my increasing number of migraines and the sleep issues. I am just so tired all of the time.

I am also angry, and I know I have to deal with it or it will kill me. It's eating away at me from the inside out. I am miserable. Going to work is my escape, just as it was when Chris was alive. I go to forget for a bit about everything swirling around me, particularly the Tur family's attacks (they have set up a hashtag to garner support for their grief). I know I am acting passive-aggressively when I post certain things on social media, but it's out of a place of fear and anger. My deepest desire is to protect my children, and people still won't leave them alone. Chris's family continues to use their images without their consent, and I hate it. I think I'm somehow proving to the world that no one can hurt me, but in reality, I feel pancaked by the betrayal, injustice, abandonment, suspicion, and my kids' pain.

I don't want Savannah and Madison to have to take care of me, so I vow to parent from an emotionally-solid place. Counseling helps.

Savannah and Madison must also deal with their feelings, ones similar to mine. They want to respond to all of the unfair and inappropriate social media posts. But I convince them to let them go. Stooping to public battles and responding to such immaturity will only prolong their agony. And I know their responses will get twisted, made out to be coming from me—as if they don't have opinions of their own.

"It's not for you to handle" I urge them. I know it's hard, and I don't realize I'm stifling their voices until much later. I am only trying to protect them and help them move on with their lives. I don't yet understand they need to have an outlet for truth to prevail. They need a place to release their own anger and fear.

Eventually, Savannah finds her outlet. GTMO utilizes a Facebook page for people who have served or lived (or currently serve or live) on base to connect. It's a social page for reminiscing about decades past, through to the present, from the opening of the installation to the present day. It's quite an extraordinary page, creating community among people of all ages who share the bond of GTMO. Kids who graduated from the GTMO high school can plan reunions, sailors who have lost touch can find each other, families who had been friends and then moved to other places can reconnect. It's very much a positive page.

Unfortunately, the Tur family joins it, even though they had never been a part of the community of GTMO. They use it to advance their theories, build support in their grief, point fingers, and unleash inappropriate commentary related to Chris's death—especially Aline. I shake my head at her audacity, knowing Chris despised her. Perhaps the most interesting part of it is that Patrice, the NCIS department head, likes all of their posts. So much for neutrality.

Savannah is outraged. She cannot reconcile the fact that they've hijacked a page meant for community and unity and are turning it into a platform and a place to pick sides. So she becomes an administrator for the Facebook page. Any time a member of Chris's family posts something inappropriate about her dad, his case, or her family, she deletes it, especially if it goes against the page's purpose of camaraderie. There is no discussion, no back-and-forth arguments. Eventually, she removes the Tur family from the page altogether. It's her way of gaining some of the control she feels they have stolen from her. They have never lived there. They don't belong on there, she determines. In the coming months and years, she would delete any comment that interferes with the friendly intent of the page. I applaud her.

Madi is still trying to find her outlet, a place from which to give voice to her internal battles and rebuild her own life. Before long, she turns to humor. It's likely more sarcasm, but it's what she needs in these moments. She's a teenager.

So in the saddest moments, we create laughter. In frustration, we make jokes. Much like surgeons hovering over their operating tables, we make light of serious times just to survive. It's a temporary coping mechanism, which eventually turns into part of our daily routine.

We know our emails, texts, phone calls, and every part of our lives are constantly under scrutiny. We believe someone is always listening. They have been for months, ever since we were forced to turn over our phones, laptops, iPods, iPads, and other electronics. We have lost trust in communicating through social media or any other online outlet. So the girls and I develop code names for attorneys and others, not because we have anything to hide, but because we've lost all privacy for no good reason at all. None of us are under investigation; we're just rolled into the entire death investigation, which continues. Madi even stops recording video feeds from her laptop by placing tape over the sensors. Our paranoia is high. It starts as a way to dispel some of our fear but then later, it would become a game. It is all just ridiculous.

Summer 2015

I realize I'm getting the short end of the stick at my job. I learn from a trusted source that there are no plans to help me advance or move me to a permanent job, no support for my career. The term I hear is "blackballed." My heart deflates. No matter where I might apply, this individual tells me I will be stuck here in Pensacola. Despite promises to find me a permanent role, I'd soon discover that a newly-retired director had put a clause in my agreement that said I could never become permanent, a clause I wouldn't know about until later and not even discovered until after the regional director had retired.

I also learn my priority placement was never signed in GTMO, which means I'm not only stuck here, I'm stuck in a GS9 role. The region tells me I should feel lucky to have anything at all. They didn't previously sign it because the case was listed as "under investigation." This angers me. The lies! I was never under investigation. Chris's death was under investigation, but that didn't have anything to do with my job. J.R. was and is being investigated. I have never been under investigation.

The lack of signature is the reason I had been set up for the limited options with no chance of advancement or permanency.

I retain my fourth attorney. The region wants to make a big deal about the "affair." *Why do we keep saying that?* I've been very adamant there was no affair. Those in the media and legal world like to throw that word around. They use it lightly. And it's not okay. It was a one-time indiscretion, a lapse in judgment in my personal (civilian) life. People think the word "affair" is easy to say. But it carries huge assumptions and ramifications. J.R. and I don't have (and didn't have) a sexual love affair. This is crazy.

There is no reason my paperwork should not have been signed, especially when these are the same people who did nothing when they became aware of my domestic violence situation prior to Chris's death, and after legal back-and-forth for the greater part of two years, I settle to avoid the constant battles. The struggle drains me of my emotional and financial capacity to keep fighting. This injustice has cost me many thousands of dollars.

During this time, I had applied for an overseas position, a director-level role in Pensacola, and they had rejected me, even though I was more qualified than those who were offered the positions. My settlement is for $1000; it's a bribe to go away. Another slap in the face.

It wouldn't be until 2017 when the region would finally sign my paperwork, and, incidentally, it would be one month too late for it to matter. Once in a GS9 position for a certain period of time, you can't advance to where you once sat. I know their timing is intentional.

Now, I have to get real about money. I'm drowning. Regarding my personal life, as we near the end of the summer 2015, I receive a message explaining that the Navy is done with all of their investigations regarding Chris, basically saying, *there's nothing more to see here.* I breathe a sigh of relief. *Finally!* Maybe we can all just move on. But that message would turn out to be a lie, too.

CHAPTER 23

LEGAL SPEAK

"Sometimes the shame is not the beatings . . . the shaming is being asked to stand judgment."
—Meena Kandasamy

NCIS tells me they have finished whatever investigation they've been leading related to Chris's death, so I request the things I need from them, specifically an official death certificate. While Chris had secretly cancelled his life insurance, I had been made aware of a pension he had earned with the Navy Exchange. Savannah is considering returning to college, and my legal bills are piling up. I could sure use that money to help with my kids' education and to settle with my attorneys.

As I wait for the death certificate to arrive, I get wind of a new NCIS investigation. NCIS joined with Philadelphia Assistant District

Attorney and Department of Justice Criminal Division Public Integrity Section Trial Attorney Mark Cipolletti, and once I left the island, they had started harassing people. I use the term harass intentionally. Friends and former colleagues tell me if someone says they don't know anything, they continue pursuing them for information. I hear they have called several individuals "liars." To top it off, they are questioning people who didn't even live on the island when Chris and I did. I am dumbfounded, and it seems to everyone I talk to that they are grasping at straws. I don't understand what bone it is they feel they need to keep chewing on.

In the past, I viewed NCIS with disrespect, and sometimes disinterest, when I worked with them. During Chris's death investigation and now, I judge them with contempt. I consider the agents mosquitoes, annoying pests who refuse to leave people alone. I wonder if they simply want to be in the limelight a bit longer—if that's their motivation. It has been a wild ride for a department used to handling less globally-relevant cases on a tiny island in the Caribbean.

It's now October, and I hear there will be a grand jury convened. *For what?* I wonder.

While at work one day, my phone records dozens of missed calls. When I reach into my purse to check my phone part-way through the day, I see them. My mom, who has been staying with Madi and me, has left frantic messages. I call her back immediately.

"What's wrong?" I ask her.

"There were agents here trying to serve subpoenas." She explains they were a bit pushy, and she had to tell them to leave—that she was the only one home. I excuse myself from the work event I am attending and race home.

On my garage door hang subpoenas for Savannah, Madison, and me to testify. That these agents and their hired legal hands want to involve my children again infuriates me. I just want my kids to resume normal lives. They don't know anything of interest related to his death—except that their father was abusive. I hire attorney number five.

Now I am tasked with figuring out how to handle work responsibilities, testify for a grand jury, and support my kids who must do the same. Savannah thinks she wants to return to school, and I know I need to find the funds to pay for it. Even though the school is working with us and we are grateful, it's still a hefty amount of money to come up with.

Speaking of the school, they have been wonderful about notifying us when people are looking for Savannah, whether it is Chris's family, news media, or legal hounds. We learn a member of Chris's family has *again* contacted the school, looking for Savannah. With this information, Savannah changes her mind—decides she doesn't want to go back to school in Pennsylvania. She doesn't think it's safe, and she's tired of being hassled by her dad's family. I can see the vulnerability in her eyes, which look worn out, filled with hopelessness. I am sad for her. I wish it didn't have to be this way, but I agree with her choice to withdraw. I had worried his family would never leave her alone, too. I'm disgusted with their games.

The first grand jury testimony is an emotional day for us. Madi is in high school, and I cannot imagine the emotions she must be battling internally. We all tell the prosecutors everything we know. When they ask me about my "affair," with J.R., I admit we had sex that night in Jacksonville. I explain it wasn't an affair but a one-time event.

I tell the grand jury why I didn't disclose the night with J.R. to NCIS back in January. I just didn't think it was relevant. At the time, I was grieving Chris's death while simultaneously dealing with his family, arrangements, and the investigation. I share that if I had known about the assault Chris made on J.R., I would have disclosed our night in Jacksonville then, but without the knowledge that even happened, I didn't think our indiscretion, our personal choices that one night, mattered. I explain to the grand jury that NCIS was notoriously unprofessional and how I viewed much of what they did as a fishing expedition. Now that there is a true legal process, there is no way I'm going to hide anything.

The girls and I respect the rules of the attorneys and the process and don't tell each other about our individual testimonies. What I do leave room for is for us to share our feelings. I cannot sit back and watch my girls hide themselves and their emotions; it's not healthy. I'm careful to keep my own emotional struggles about Chris to myself. He was their dad. I won't bad mouth him past what they are already aware of because they lived through it. I allow them to be angry—because they are—and I let them be sad and confused, too. We all know he was no martyr or hero, but I want them to also remember that he was there for them in ways dads should be—coaching their games, attending their school events, and more. While I don't sugarcoat anything, and I answer most of the girls' questions about our marriage, it's difficult to keep so much to myself. In the end, it's what a mother must do. I didn't want them to take my anger and make it their anger. They have enough of their own emotional rides to navigate.

December 3, 2015

I am summoned back to Jacksonville for more grand jury testimony. This time, I am required to face the jury in person rather than through privately recorded testimonies. I go alone, with the exception of my lawyer. No girls. No mom. Just me. I had flown everyone down for the first appearance, including my attorney from the D.C. area, since the girls had to testify that time. It was costly!

This time, I drive, still not a fan of flying. I only have to cover the expense of getting my attorney there.

I find out my friend, Kelly, who has been one of my closest friends alongside Dawnell, is also appearing before the grand jury on the same day. She has since taken another job as a public affairs officer and has moved on from GTMO. We have been exchanging social media messages for a while, particularly as NCIS agents continued their bizarre questions. She had been targeted numerous times. My birthday passed a couple weeks ago, and Kelly had sent me a celebratory message.

When I arrive at the hotel, I unpack and step outside for a cigarette. Kelly arrives from the airport, and as she passes by, we agree to meet in a bit for a drink to catch up. She never shows up. Kelly is like that, sometimes, so I don't think much of it. I chalk it up to delayed flights and fatigue and assume she might be working in her room.

The next morning, I head over to the courthouse to give my testimony. I've never been in front of a grand jury before—never stepped foot in a courtroom or even had a traffic ticket—and I don't know what to expect, perhaps a TV-drama-style courtroom? Even without expectations, what I encounter is odd and intimidating. Let's just say, they really "church" it up on TV. I enter a drab, plain-Jane room with no windows. As I'm ushered in, without my attorney by the way, I notice the judge, the jury, the assistant attorney general, and a court reporter. I only learned minutes ago that my attorney stays outside the sealed, sound-proof room. I feel completely alone.

I sit where they direct me, where all eyes are on me.

"Do you swear to tell the truth . . ."

I state my name and then they pummel me with questions. I had somewhat of a briefing on what the questions will be, but they still intimate me. Everyone stares, and I briefly think, "They are literally judging me."

I believe the questions are slanted and offer me no opportunity to expand or explain, which I realize is normal, but I also know I'm not on trial here. I get the sense that no matter what I say, everyone has already made up their minds about me. It's an awful place to be. *Caged again.*

Other questions seem weird, and I wonder why the answers to them matter at all, such as, "Why didn't you attend Chris's funeral service in Pennsylvania?"

It's an unfair question. I attempt to share that it had been canceled, that it was planned by Chris's family, and how inappropriate the service would have been . . . how the service in GTMO was the one that mattered most to the girls and me because that was our family, those were our friends. I don't think anyone cares about the *why*. All the jury members hear is that I didn't attend my husband's funeral.

The assistant AG already knows I'm going to plead the fifth when asked a certain question about J.R. He asks anyway. When it lands on me, I laugh. *Why am I laughing?* I cannot control myself. I realize it's likely my body reacting to the stress, a coping mechanism of sorts, but I know others must be thinking I'm a terrible person. There is nothing funny about the question, this situation, or Chris's death, but I just can't help it. *Oh my gosh, stop it, Lara!* I bite the side of my cheek to make myself stop. My mouth is laughing, and my heart is crying. I cannot believe this is happening, and I feel ashamed.

If it's possible to pray and talk at the same time, that's what I do. I just want this to be over. We get to the end, and I am excused briefly. They want to discuss my answers—talk behind my back—and then bring me back in. I keep thinking this is cruel for someone who's not on trial.

Months and years later, there would be two questions that stick out, ones I can't forget. They both produced such a high level of shame that I wanted to vomit. One had to do with our early marriage when I had secured protective orders under the claim of child and spousal abuse but had then let Chris back into our home and lives. It was a question that sat heavily on my heart. Without knowing the details or intricacies of what it's like to be an abused spouse and mother, held captive by financial worries, it's impossible to understand my perspective. It was such a shame-filled question, and when it was asked, I did everything I could to remind myself that I was a good mother. I hated that they tried to put the blame on me. Chris was the abuser. Chris controlled everything. I was the victim. No one understood.

The other question I will never forget: "Mrs. Tur, what are your degrees in?" *Why does that matter?* Oh. I get it. You think I could have counseled my husband? You believe I should have been able to use my education to fix this? To make him stop? To change his addictive and violent behavior? *I see.*

My perspective, sitting in that little room, is that the questions are meant to point to me as the problem, or at the very least, blame me for Chris's ongoing behavior. At least that is how I take them. I become defensive. Shame morphs into anger. Again, anger is easier to feel because it gives me the false sense of control in a room where I have no control whatsoever.

I leave feeling bad about myself. I go home exhausted.

2016 is not much better on the legal front. Privacy is still a lost commodity. They ask me for everything. They track my phone, emails, and social media. I even swab my mouth and send them my DNA. I wonder when it will all end so the girls and I can finally move on. It's been a year.

The Tur family members continue to feed their narrative to anyone who will listen, including a Facebook page "dedicated" to military corruption, similar in style (and truth) to *The National Inquirer.*

Savannah doesn't want to be associated with the Turs any longer. She legally changes her name.

In October, I follow suit and legally change mine back to my maiden name. It doesn't take long before people leak that to the media, as well. Madison forges a different path. Her opinion is that the Tur name is what she was born with and no one, no matter how ridiculous or unjust they act, should be able to steal that from her. "It's not about them. It's not about dad. It's about me." So she chooses to keep the Tur name.

I applaud both girls' paths. They are fiercely independent thinkers, and I am grateful they have found their voices.

———————

I finally get some of my items back from NCIS. (It would be October 2020 before I get the remainder of my items back. Though I will never be sure. I was not home when they searched my house, and they returned things piece by piece over five years.)

I have an "off the record" conversation with one of the agents there.

"Why are you being so defensive?" he asks.

"What else do you want me to be? I feel attacked from every angle. Tell me, who is *not* attacking me?" I say. "It's been almost two years, and I haven't had a chance to grieve. My children are being attacked, too. How would you like me to feel?"

This agent is blunt. He looks at me and says, "This isn't about you. It's about a man who died, and you're making it about you."

I can't help but chuckle. "That is *my point* exactly. In all of this, it's like Chris walks six inches above the water with Jesus. It's simply not true. You're right. It's not about me. It's not about my girls. Yet I keep getting subpoenaed. My girls have to go in hiding. I am made out to be the enemy. Yes, I agree with you. It's not even about me."

It is a frustrating conversation. It rolls around to why I plead the fifth if I have nothing to hide.

"It seems like you're protecting someone," he argues.

"Yeah, I *am* protecting someone. Two people. My children. I am a single mom now. I don't want all this to affect my job! I have to provide for our family now. I need immunity."

"You think it will affect your job?"

"Yes! That's the exact reason I do what I do! I have bills to pay," I say. My face contorts in hopeful desperation. *Why can't people see this? My career has already been affected! I've already been black-balled!*

I hope this becomes a light-bulb moment for this NCIS agent, that he now understands I'm not trying to hide anything. I'm simply a protective mother, one whose career has already been affected.

"People need to stop making this out to be some Hallmark movie," I say. "That's so stupid. We're not trying to ride off into the sunset. J.R. was my friend. That's it."

"We're only here to understand how Chris died. Why are you making it so hard?

"Chris was my husband. I didn't even know he had died before NCIS was asking me questions. It's been almost two years of questions. Stop making it hard for *me and my children*. I'm trying to work with you. I'm an open book as long as I can provide for my kids."

It's December 14, 2016, and subpoenas are dished out again. Only now, there is a new trial attorney for the Public Integrity Section, Criminal Division. This will prove important because first of all, I am no longer being served papers on my garage door. Communication is going through my attorney—privately.

I have always cooperated with all the investigations and the legal process. Finally, I am afforded a little bit more respect. The gentleman who takes over has a different way about him. He is kind; not aggressive but compassionate. He's the complete opposite of his predecessor. I don't get the impression he's assuming the worst about me. His assistant is the same way. Whether this new team is simply using smoke and mirrors, I don't know. I hope not.

There have always been moments in time when the Tur family has had a leg up on information, and I have been the last to know. I've had to go to my attorney to find out details about the investigation or process after discovering them on social media.

The reasons are flimsy: "Well, you're a witness," is an excuse that is wearing thin. But now, there is a different air in the room this time, during my new grand jury testimony. I feel the new trial attorneys are listening to understand, not to throw me under the bus. Maybe I am naïve, but I am more relaxed. I don't feel the waves of self-defensiveness that I felt in previous months.

They provide me with details about becoming a protective witness and a victim's program, which the girls and I join. I hear them, but I can't follow all the information. People believe an indictment against J.R. is coming soon. I am sad for J.R. I'm sad for his family. Later, I will have to process so many emotions. I don't feel any punishment is right in this case. He didn't show up at Chris's house and assault him in the middle of the night.

During the proceeding, I hear someone say, "If you want protection from anyone contacting you—" My ears perk up, and I interrupt him.

"The only people I'm concerned about are Chris's family members."

Everyone says they believe the indictment will give the Tur family the closure they seek. "Maybe it will allow you all to heal and reconcile—"

"No, that ship has sailed," I say. "If you've been dealing with them at all, you know they are crazy. Please don't insult me. You know all about them and their lies. Do not even think about us reconciling."

There is no chance for that.

CHAPTER 24
TODAY

"Each time a woman stands up for herself without knowing it, possibly without claiming it, she stands up for all women."
—Maya Angelou

One night, the girls sit me down.

"Mom, we want you to know something," they say. "We are going to move on eventually, and we don't want you to be alone. We have our whole lives ahead of us. You don't need our permission, but if you're waiting for it, we want you to know you can start seeing other people. It's okay. We want you to be happy."

I am struck by their hearts for me. I know they are growing up fast, but this blows me away. I am approaching my fortieth birthday. I haven't dated since I was nineteen years old.

My girls introduce me to dating apps and even teach me how to stay safe. I laugh. Savannah, Madi, and I are growing closer with each passing month.

I end up meeting someone as the days march toward the holidays. I am not looking for a tomorrow, only for a today where I can remember what it's like to have fun again. Sometimes, I am afraid I've forgotten how to enjoy life. This person makes me laugh. He takes my mind off of everything else going on. He isn't affiliated with the government or the military, and that gives me a measure of relief. I'm looking for honesty and integrity. He knows the story and the battles I continue to wage, and he accepts them. I can't hide who I am, and I don't lie, so I'm glad he's okay with it all.

When I'm with him, there is no leash of expectation. As time goes by, I learn I can think about tomorrow when I'm ready. This relationship is a nice distraction and, in some ways, the fulfilment of the fantasy I had lived out in that hotel room in Florida. There is no degradation. No fear. No abuse. It's a season where I feel I might be able to usher hope back into my life. Something I haven't felt in decades.

Personally, I am learning how to manage all these lows in my life without letting one or two suffocate me. I believe I'm getting better at compartmentalizing. My work is work, and my home life is filled with family and friends. I finally have a healthier mindset.

When 2016 arrives, I feel stronger than I've felt in years. I see things more clearly, and can task life better. Emotionally and physically, I'm whole again. I have a different outlook on life, one that I had been thinking was impossible. Now, I'm making it a reality. I'm no longer a victim living in a victim's mindset. I'm me—a survivor who was victimized, but is now able to view myself with empathy and compassion. I snap out of all the negative thinking that once held me back. I've stopped putting so much weight and significance on the things I can't change and focus on what is important to me—what makes me happy. This. This is the type of role model I have always wanted to be for my daughters.

———————

Late Fall 2018

We're still waiting for the legal process to end. People had assumed an indictment was coming back in 2016. One didn't. Both of my girls are in college, Madison out of state and Savannah in Florida. I cherish the fact we're all still close, even though Madi is a three-hour drive away. She chose to study criminal justice, and she's thriving. My heart swells as she finds her calling. Now, each of us has found her control piece, a way to handle things, specifically Chris's family's antics.

Then it happens. A car accident. Someone hits me, and it's severe enough that I am forced to medically retire from the government. I can't drive, and I will have long-term difficulties, ones that will affect my daily life. My doctors say the years of physical and emotional abuse I sustained will impair my ability to heal. Hearing the doctors tell me the damage is likely permanent because it wasn't my first concussion, makes for a disheartening and difficult day.

For the next two years, I'll be in and out of various medical procedures.

January 8, 2019

My work-life balance is still good. I am surrounded by family—my parents have retired to Florida—and I have made great friends. I'm still involved with that special someone, a life partner for sure, and I feel like I've hit a point in my life where I am making all my decisions for myself. They are my choices. I have boundaries, and I'm no longer feeling caged by others. Though, honestly, the cage will be with me forever. It's easy to feel safe inside it after so many years banging on the bars to be released.

When it finally happened, I assume it was similar to a long-term inmate being released to the outside world. I feel at times alone and suspicious.

I want to believe the good in people. I just can't trust them. Friendships are difficult and slow to build. Kelly and I are estranged. Dawnell and I don't talk. The heartbreak of betrayal from those I loved cuts deep. I'm not sure I find much value in friends, and I know it's a cynical stance to take. I think I fear it's just a matter of time before one leaves. So in that regard, the cage keeps the walls up around my heart— keeps people at arm's length. It's a point of control, stemming from my experiences. The keeper of the cage is me, and there are times I want to run back in, lock the door, and wilt away.

Today, the indictment comes through. J.R. is publicly arrested and then released. I see it on Facebook of all places! I had asked everyone to notify me before something like this might happen so that I could protect my girls. They are on college campuses, and I don't want the news to blindside them, or worse, the media to show up and hound them.

No one had notified me. I frantically call Madison, leaving her a message to drive home and not to look on social media. I hate that it has to be like this—again. I am angry, incensed that my attorney finally calls, after the fact. *What happened to the protective victim's program?*

I have no idea how big the media story will be, so I want my girls close. Once they are home, we spend the weekend holed up and waiting. Thankfully, we are not harassed. The whole story is abbreviated, but our emotions, even our bodies, are responding like we're right back in 2015 again.

―――――――

It's May. Madison and I are served with paperwork from an estate attorney in Florida, claiming the Tur family is seeking oversight and representation of Chris's estate. The girls are to be named as beneficiaries, and they are attempting to cut me out altogether.

I find this both ludicrous and interesting since I had closed out Chris's estate in Virginia, our permanent residence at the time of his death, nearly five years before. And I'm shocked his family could even try such a thing since I was his wife at the time of his death. Don't spouses take precedence?

Apparently, Aline and Mike opened an estate in Florida and became executors of Chris's estate there. Somehow, the outcome of this fiasco is just as ridiculous as the attempt. With my head injuries, I'm unable to think through this, let alone fight it. Aline and Mike are somewhat successful. The girls are outraged that a woman whom they don't know and whom Chris hated now has control of his assets.

"How can she represent Dad's estate when he wouldn't even say her name when he was alive?" Madison asks. I have no answers. I, too, find it curious that the legal landscape, the very one that declared Mike unfit to handle financial situations or return to work after a car accident he experienced before Chris's death, is able to push me out and take over Chris's estate.

But I just want to move on, and I encourage the girls to do the same.

In late 2019, Madison and I are subpoenaed by the prosecution for the January 2020 trial of J.R. I beg them to only include Madison if needed. She is heading back to school in early January, and I am done with her life being upended by all this legal and family chaos. She wasn't at J.R.'s house that night when Chris attacked him. I ask them to only call her to testify if they need to hear (again) about her life with Chris as her dad through the years.

I am given all my transcripts and provided with intense run-throughs with the prosecution team the November before the trial.

Because of my car accident that caused, among other injuries, a head injury, and my short-term memory has been affected, I am granted the opportunity to have any questions forwarded to me ahead of time. There are more run-throughs in January in Jacksonville before the trial begins.

I don't want to show any weakness, especially in a courtroom full of people who seem to focus so much energy and life's work on judging my every move and every word that comes through my mouth. It's the same reason I won't take my pain medications: to give no one any doubts about the clarity and truthfulness of my words.

I'm also given the medical authorization to have my parents drive me to Jacksonville. Because I'm under medical care, they have to be added to the orders to travel so I can appear before the jury.

I don't want my partner to come. He is willing and always emphatic, but I just don't want to mix my current life with this former one. I want to keep the new life I've worked so hard to build separate from everything of the past, most especially the Tur family.

I learn that Dawnell has been subpoenaed, as well. She and I request permission to remain distanced from the Turs. Madison, if needed at the trial, doesn't want to be cornered like Savannah had been in the past.

"They really have no filter," I say. I am worried about what they might put on their social media pages, especially if they take photos of Madi or me or confront me in public. I am not concerned about J.R.'s family.

The prosecution, the investigators, my legal team, and my parents all agree there are security concerns, and we are put up in a hotel away from the Tur family, the media, and everyone else. The agents assigned to protect me from the Tur family and any contact they try to make with me advise us to avoid the general area where the family is staying and any surrounding restaurants they may eat. I agree and abide by their request. I don't want any drama.

My testimony has never changed or even wavered. I am able to sit on the stand and tell my story, again, without anyone to support me in the courtroom, which I'm okay with at this point. I don't want my parents there because they know who I am, what has happened, and the mess that is this story. I don't want to put them through another emotional testimony. After telling my side so many times now, I have shut down some of my own feelings about it as well. Or, maybe my emotions have been maxed out.

After I'm finished, my legs are shaky as I make my way out of the courtroom. I wipe my face. It feels sweaty. Depleted of all energy, I hope I am finished. I hope they don't call me back for more. Because of that cracked door, the slight possibility I'll be asked to return, I am advised not to attend the trial, not to sit in the galley. I understand the reason: that I may be called back as a witness, and no one wants my testimony influenced by what I hear during the trial. I get that. What I don't understand is the other reason the legal teams provide:

"We don't want jury members looking at you as the widow and making decisions or forming opinions based on your facial expressions."

I think about that for a long time. *Maybe that's appropriate. But then, am I not allowed to hear what others say? Don't I have that right? But I don't want to negatively influence jury members. This is all bad enough . . . I don't know.*

In the end, I follow the advice of everyone and skip the rest of the trial. That night, I eat dinner with my parents and Dawnell before we make our way home. I check the media pages and the Tur's Facebook pages to see if any news has hit the Internet, particularly about my testimony. The family is unusually quiet. I see they have posted a note saying they will refrain from any posting of stories or commentary until the trial is over. But in the next breath, I see a story.

The Tur family posts a story about me wiping my forehead as I exit the courtroom. Underneath, they claim I had flipped them off with my middle finger. I guess they couldn't help themselves and had to post something. With a red background, they write, "What has not been lost in this moment is that Christopher would be alive and well today if Lara was faithful to her husband and loyal to her children."

"What?" It's such an absurd accusation. I was flanked by my NCIS agent and my court-appointed attorney. There was no reason, nor any way, I could have been so profane. Rather, they are the ones who are vulgar. Many of their posts include name-calling, how I'm a "bi—," "whore," "skank," and more. In public places. I don't see how this helps their grief or their cause. And I would love to discuss spousal faithfulness after discovering some of Chris's medical records, how he had been treated for STDs overseas, after we were married, while I was home pregnant with Savannah. But I don't respond.

Everyone at dinner realizes that if I breathe wrong, the Tur family will take offense. I can do nothing "right" in their eyes, nor is there anything I can do that won't be misrepresented. They make everything about them, and the word "narcissistic" is used as we discuss it over our meal. I brush it off as we laugh at their expense. I just have to. A middle finger? Really? Though, later, I would tell my attorney about it just so he is aware of the continued harassment. I want to let it all go, but I can't.

I travel home and wade through the days as the trial continues without me. I would later regret that choice.

Through friends, news reports, and social media, I learn how multiple people who took the stand to talk about the night of the Hail and Farewell had committed perjury. They blatantly lied in what I can only assume was an attempt to save themselves, their careers, or their reputations. On that stand, people took oaths and lied about how much they had to drink, what they drank, and how much help they provided that night. There were some pretty big whoppers told in that courtroom, so maybe it's a good thing I wasn't there. I am not sure I could have stopped myself from standing up and yelling, "Objection," or something foolish. I do wish the jury members had seen my face when those "witnesses" sat on that stand and ignored the truth.

I just can't take the lies any more. They are so numerous, and they're being told by so many, and it's been years since anyone has heard only the truth—lies from the Tur family, the XO on the base, and others. People I used to call friends. The feeling of being caged returns. I am held in this unending prison where reality has been set aside in vain efforts to protect a few undeserving individuals and a whole military base on the tiny island of Cuba.

––––––––––

With J.R.'s case, ten charges are dropped to eight, and he is found guilty on six. One of the charges that he is found not guilty is the one related to adultery. The three of us, Savannah, Madi, and I, are asked if we want to make our own statements, and we decline. It's a circus. The drama is not worth it. Plus, statements are usually made against the defendant, and honestly, I have nothing to say against J.R. I don't feel this whole process has been a true carriage of justice. I may be naïve. Maybe it's denial.

The Tur family makes a statement. I think my daughters are going to pass out when they hear it. It's dramatic and emotional. They say things, such as, "Chris was such a good dad and husband and brother." They talk about how his reputation was smeared. Worst of all, they make the statement on behalf of the girls, too. Savannah and Madi are beside themselves, trying to manage the lack of boundaries the Tur family exhibits and the audacity they show as they include them in their statement. Aline always seems to be the one speaking—the only one whom Chris despised. I just don't get it. (I still don't understand, even to the present day.)

Months pass and now COVID-19 is spreading like wildfire around the globe. The sentencing is pushed to October 8, 2020.

I don't begrudge the Tur family for grieving. I resent the fact that with all these public shenanigans, they stole the grieving process from my daughters and me. From day one, when I learned Chris was dead, they never stopped pushing. The three of us haven't had the opportunity to properly mourn, and we have been harshly judged about issues they know nothing about.

That's not necessarily accurate. Ann, Chris's mom, knew about Chris's behavior. She had heard his outbursts, seen the holes in the walls, and come to my rescue in the past. She knows he was not an Iraqi soldier, home with PTSD. His behavior was not a result of combat or memories of war. He never served in the Middle East. His alcoholism, drug use, and angry outbursts had started well before any deployment to Haiti or Japan to live on a base or a boat. I have learned a mother will protect her child, even when the child is a grown man abusing his family.

From the beginning, people have treated me like a little girl in a corner, never telling me the whole truth about what happened, what they discovered in the course of all their investigations, or keeping me in the dark about the newest legal maneuvers. I ask questions, but there are not (and never have been) any full answers. Even though I was Chris's wife, I have never been read into the full details. Somehow, the loudest voices—the Tur family's voices—have been given that courtesy, which they have turned into their own shaming platform.

The Chris they present to the world is not the Chris I knew. The man I married was an insecure, troubled individual who dealt with alcohol-related issues for the duration of our marriage. He hid things from me, consistently lied to me and others, and abused me—not just physically, but emotionally and financially.

I am told by everyone who has information related to his death and this case, "Be careful because you don't want people to look at you as a bitter widow. You don't want people to think you had something to do with this." It's an unfair position to put me in. And I'm not the only one who's backed into the corner. There are thousands of us.

———————

Like so many other women and children in homes where there is domestic abuse and violence, we have been made out to be the ones at fault. Much like those two questions in my grand jury testimony that haunt me, aimed to put blame on my shoulders, people often ask, "Why didn't you schedule the girls for counseling?"

In a system where there is no support, in a place where people have turned their backs on them—and on their mom—in a world where we are criticized for speaking out, why would they desire, why would I subject them to, asking for help from that same system?

If we yell just as loudly as the other side, would people really hear us? With those warnings to "stay quiet," and "don't rock the boat," I have been trapped, caged on all sides, for a long time now. My girls desperately want to fight back in the public eye, but I ask them not to. It's the only time I have ever told my girls what to do. I have never advised them about relationships—whom to cut out, whom to trust, or with whom to reconcile. They are grown women. They need to make those choices on their own. But when they want to defend me and my reputation against the lies, I ask them not to.

There are silent women and children everywhere, ones living with abusive partners. I'm thinking particularly about the ones who work in the government or serve through the military, but there are other environments just as challenging. I don't understand how those who are being victimized are asked to be quiet or even silenced in the midst of their requests for help.

The Tur family has crucified me in the public eye. NCIS has thrown me into a washing machine on full cycle, even though I have never been accused of anything. I have done nothing wrong (apart from one instance of adultery) and was not part of my husband's death in any way. I was abused, and on that horrific night, asked for help to no avail.

Chris, on the other hand, was treated for STDs while in Japan, unfaithful to me from the beginning. Just because Chris died doesn't mean I can't express my feelings or tell the truth about what life under our roof was like. It doesn't mean I wanted him dead either. The truth doesn't mean I hated him. My desire to speak out against the injustice or the domestic violence and lack of resources doesn't mean I am a bad person or did anything wrong. And I can't—I won't—just forget about it all.

I spent twenty years with this man. For the last couple months of his life, I had this idea that we would get divorced, that we'd both live on base in separate houses so Madi could graduate with her friends, that we'd both keep working at our jobs at GTMO, and it would all be okay. Maybe this was a naïve notion, unrealistic on my part. But others had done this, so I didn't believe it was that far-fetched an idea. I didn't hate Chris. I hated living with him as his wife because I hated what he did to me. I just couldn't live with him anymore, and I wanted him to get the help he needed . . . to get healthy, to live his life to the fullest, too. I loved Chris. I loved him very much. You can't spend two decades with someone, have a family with someone, and not love them on some level. A lack of love for Chris wasn't the problem. I didn't say, "I do," on our wedding day because I thought Chris was perfect. I had been willing to try to work things out, up until nearly the very end.

I think Chris's family believes a lack of love was the issue, that I wanted to hurt him or leave him for someone else. That's a false narrative they have created, perhaps to quiet their own inner consciences, the ones that know what kind of person Chris had become. He was getting so reckless and his behavior was bleeding into every aspect of our lives, not just our marriage. I could no longer function. I could no longer breathe. I didn't want a divorce to start a new relationship with someone else. I wanted it to start over with myself, to rediscover my strengths, and to remember that I am a capable and lovable person.

You know, I still have conversations with Chris in my head. I am still angry that he's not here. I'm frustrated that he left this world and this mess behind. I am often sad that he is missing such big milestones in our girls' lives. He is missing graduations, and he isn't here to walk either one down the aisle if and when they get married. I'm sad for our daughters. He stole those moments from them when he lost control that life-changing night (and all those times leading up to that night). He could have been here if he had gotten the help he needed—the help, honestly, that he deserved.

I can't think of a good reason for this ending. I wrestle with all of this—even today. I wrestle with the fact his family has destroyed relationships between Savannah and Madison and themselves. I don't know why the Tur family is so angry with me and so focused on ruining my reputation. I don't know where they think that will get them, what their end game is. I don't know why they think the girls would ever choose them over me after all they've done to disrupt truth and trust. We didn't have to be friends, but we could have had a civil relationship for the girls' sake. Demonizing me ruined that opportunity. They will never get that opportunity back. There isn't a dollar amount in the world that would persuade Savannah and Madi to reconcile with them. And I know Chris would not have wanted it this way. It's terrible. And it's so very sad.

I don't have any ill will or feelings toward my nieces or nephews. I don't believe any of the children (now all nearly grown or teenagers) should have ever been involved in this mess, no matter in which household they live(d). I hope they can be independent thinkers and not fall into any one opinion or another because of the conversations and feelings presented by the adults in their homes. I know I've tried hard to do that for my girls, encouraging them to make choices for themselves.

It's a shame that a family was torn apart like this. There are no happy endings here.

An abusive marriage. One tragic evening. In four hours, everything was consumed. A man died. Relationships were broken. People were changed. Lives were forever altered.

I have changed. My outlook has changed. Even my body chemistry has changed. I view myself differently now. That is one blessing, but there are so many tragedies. My daughters look at the whole world differently now . . . and they always will.

December 2020

I own my home, and financially, no one is threatening to cut off my security. No one is saying, "I'm going to take this from you if you don't do what I say." There are no impossible expectations looming over me, including any I've put on myself. I live free, never to be held back or held down by anyone again. I no longer worry about tomorrow. I want to be careful—to never lose sight of "me" again.

Healthwise, I have a lot to overcome from the accident. But I remain thankful for the recent years because I have worked to establish my own sense of security and safety and stand on my own two feet. I am where I am for no other reason than because I worked hard to overcome everything that has happened. And because a few people stood by me (and still do), reminding me that I'm worth it.

CHAPTER 25

A PLEA FOR CHANGE

"The more that we choose not to talk about domestic violence, the more we shy away from the issue, the more we lose."
—Russell Wilson

There is a systemic problem when those who are abused are kept from information, unaided by the "powers that be," and asked to stay quiet. There are a lot of women living like this right now—women living secret lives, stuck in situations just like the marriage and life I was stuck in.

There are others learning the same script Chris taught me: You aren't good enough. You can't do this without me. I am in charge. There are thousands of spouses, thousands of abuse survivors, who have not received the support they need. The details may vary, but the general cage is the same. They are stuck between these limiting beliefs and hope. They are handcuffed in financial jail with a spouse who keeps the lock and key. They get pregnant before they are married. They have children to think about. Like me, they can't see any way out.

Abuse within the military and government is a silent epidemic. Even though we were civilians, we lived on a naval base and the government was my employer. Many commanders believe it's more important to salvage a soldier's military career than ensure an abused spouse's safety. It's a harsh reality. On the flip side, specifically to this case, my friend is paying the price for his silence, punished by a system where there is no hope for a woman like me, one caught between two large systems. J.R. honored my wish and didn't report Chris's abuse. Had he done so, his life would likely be different today, but I cannot imagine what mine would be like. The civilian spouse, the government employee, is not a protected individual.

Another reality—abuse among military couples and those living on military installations is wildly underreported. Victims often fear repercussions from their abusers, particularly since they are trained for battle and often carry weapons, should they be demoted—but not arrested—as a result of the report of abuse. There are no safe havens, secret houses for women and children to run to, in the military.

Aside from the physical harm victims fear, spouses fear financial ruin. They have been taught through the years that they cannot parent alone, provide for their families, or survive the sure-to-follow financial hardships. The current monthly payment a spouse is entitled to if her husband is discharged from the military because of an abuse offense is $1,125. That's poverty-level income. And sponsorship—housing, career, and benefits, such as access to counseling—is all forfeited.

Change must happen. We cannot tolerate so many people feeling trapped by their domestic situations and because they live on—or support those who live on—a military base. We must do better. My story is not that unusual. I am not an outlier. The only difference is that my story made headline news.

As of 2020, the government posts guidelines for employees and managers on domestic violence for review on their website. The online guidebook, which provides a small notation that it is there for all those affected by DV, feels inadequate. Most of the DV works cited come from the '90s, offering hand-off advice: see it, say it, and find someone else to deal with it before it becomes our problem to handle. The majority of people affected by DV are women. Therefore, the guide is written only to women and to managers dealing with female victims. The recommendation is for women to seek outside counseling and directs managers to offer work-at-home options if their staff member is missing too much work due to her situation.

What we all lose sight of is that military members and government employees (such as I was) work for the American public. Civilians and government employees on installations in the U.S. and around the world are the support community for the military. Without the same work-life balance measures we find in the corporate world, there is never going to be cohesive support network for our military members. It's currently a "Do as I say, not as I do" mentality. How can a civilian government member effectively counsel a military member if they have no one to turn to and are in turmoil themselves? Provisions of 1-800 numbers and links to peruse hardly provide protection for men and women in both government and military positions, serving in the United States and around the world.

While government employees have no avenue and no true support, military spouses find their reporting systems in a fight for legitimacy. In the Navy, spouses must fulfill a "criteria" in a committee if the DV is "enough to count." What does that mean? It means *is it enough for someone to do something? Is it enough for someone to step in to prevent visible or permanent harm? Is it enough to ruin a military career over?* And who is "someone?" The chain of command? The government in general? The lack of concrete definitions and policies is alarming.

Prosecution rates are unknown. In January 2019, the military made DV punishable under the UCMJ (Uniform Code of Military Justice). If the spouse does not meet the government's criteria for DV, there is no support. The abused spouse is spit back into their home and becomes alone in their world—again.

Domestic violence support should be available to all members of the military, government, and their dependents without worry of reprisal, without having to fit into "someone's" quotas for criteria, without worry of rank, and without issue about whom anyone works for. Program changes need to be made for the safety of those who sacrifice for our country, for those under residential roofs and across the halls at work, even though they're not in action, holding weapons. Program changes need to be made so people feel safe to come forward. No one should wait to report abuse. No one should fear freedom.

There should be no more cages.

AFTERWORD

I have been repeatedly asked one question by friends—ex-friends now—prosecutors, defense attorneys, and others through the years. I want to address it here.

Am I in love with J.R.?

To me, the answer is, and has always been, far more complicated than anyone could ever understand. Most won't value me or my answer enough to hear me, to listen without judgment, especially when the reasons they ask always have ulterior motives. I think there is value in truth, so I choose to address it here.

I have loved J.R. since the moment he asked me to dance at the Admiral's Call. I don't love him in the salacious sense that everyone seems to assume. I have loved and will love him for the respect he showed me and will be forever grateful to him for helping me see *me*. There is no greater gravity of emotion, no better words I can use, to explain how I feel when I think of him. I have often answered *no, I don't love him* because I believe people don't listen to me when I try to explain this; people hear what they want to hear. They (the media, Chris's family, prosecutors, and others) believe I am pining over J.R. or am *in love* with him. Or they assume I am trying to protect "the Captain." None of this is true.

I continue to carry a large measure of guilt that J.R. has paid substantial consequences for a man who was spiraling out of control long before J.R. ever met either of us.

The truth is: Without J.R., I don't know where I would be today. He showed me what would be possible if I could muster just an ounce of self-love and the resolve to fight for something better for myself and my girls.

In the end, the only people I will forever protect are my daughters. But that will never detract from my gratitude to those who have been undeniable pillars throughout my process, people such as Amy, Kristie, my parents . . . and of course, now, my grown girls.

ABOUT THE AUTHOR

Lara Sabanosh has dedicated her life to helping others. Beginning in her youth as a volunteer and continuing throughout her career, she has counseled families, individuals, and children—civilian and military—in finding and reaching their emotional, educational, or professional goals. She's found joy in helping others become their best selves. Lara holds two ABD doctorates in Research and Evaluation, as well as Clinical Psychology.

Lara has since retired. Her new goal? To continue to help others through the written word.

She hopes that by sharing her story, she will bring a voice and awareness to the topics of domestic abuse and a broken system in desperate need of repair.

Throughout Lara's journey, there has been one constant: the pride, respect, and unconditional love that she has for her daughters. These intelligent young women have overcome the same traumatic challenges described within Caged. They have used those experiences to help forge who they are and are currently in the process of completing their educational journeys to advance into careers that help others.

Lara now spends her time in Pensacola, Florida with her loving family, dogs, and grand puppies.

She's learning to move forward and one day hopes to find closure and will no longer be caged by her past.

A free ebook edition is available with the purchase of this book.

To claim your free ebook edition:

Visit MorganJamesBOGO.com
Sign your name CLEARLY in the space
Complete the form and submit a photo of
the entire copyright page
You or your friend can download the ebook
to your preferred device

A **FREE** ebook edition is available for you
or a friend with the purchase of this print book.

CLEARLY SIGN YOUR NAME ABOVE

Instructions to claim your free ebook edition:
1. Visit MorganJamesBOGO.com
2. Sign your name CLEARLY in the space above
3. Complete the form and submit a photo
   of this entire page
4. You or your friend can download the ebook
   to your preferred device

Print & Digital Together Forever.

Snap a photo

Free ebook

Read anywhere

CPSIA information can be obtained
at www.ICGtesting.com
Printed in the USA
JSHW020024091121
20315JS00001B/18